KATE BRACKS *The sweet life*

KATE BRACKS

The sweet life

the basics   and beyond ...

EBURY
PRESS

Contents

For the people I love most in this world:
Luke, Erin, Liam and Maya.

Author's note

Most people cook savoury food, if for nothing else but to feed themselves on a daily basis. This simple fact means that most people are practised in at least some of the basics of savoury cooking. When it comes to cooking desserts and sweets, however, many people are nervous and opt to purchase something ready-made to finish off a meal, while others love to cook desserts and sweets often.

My theory is that practice makes perfect (or close enough to be delicious), but often we expect that the first time we make something new it will be faultless. My plea with you is to be patient with yourself, especially if you have not done much cooking of desserts and sweets.

My hope is that this book will be a useful tool for any home cook, whether beginner or experienced. I have designed the pages so that each chapter starts with a few recipes which represent 'the basics' for a particular dessert-making technique. Once these are mastered, the techniques can be built upon to cook the recipes in the 'beyond the basics' section. For the more creative home cooks there are also notes along the way of how you can take the recipes in different directions for yourself. Of course, these are all in the realm of home cooking, for we are home cooks!

In recognition that people are at different stages in their own culinary journey, I've also included a code to help you determine which recipes are most suited to your cooking desires and abilities. You will see it at the beginning of each title.

recipes that are simple and relatively quick to master

recipes that require a little bit more effort but are still very achievable

recipes that involve more processes and therefore more time and effort

for the avid home cook who wants a bit more of a challenge

Whether new to cooking or more experienced, here are a few helpful things to know:

Every oven is different. The times and temperatures given in the recipes are a good guide, but in the end you as the cook need to make the final judgment call. I discovered recently that my relatively new oven is 10°C out, and if I hadn't been in need of checking it for recipe-writing purposes I would probably never have known! Some ovens have 'hot spots', so you need to learn where they are and respond appropriately. If you're cooking meringue-based desserts your oven will need to have a good seal.

Ingredients differ. The brand, season in which they are produced and packaged, and the weather on the day of cooking, can all have an impact on the dish you're making. Again, the recipe is a very good guide but you may need to adjust it slightly to accommodate the circumstances in which you're cooking.

Eggs come in all different sizes. For the purposes of this cookbook I've used 59g eggs, but I do find that when I'm cooking I use whatever I have to hand (which at this stage is whatever my chooks have laid!), and I find that on most occasions it makes little difference.

Most dessert cooks use unsalted butter. I actually prefer to use salted butter as I find my own additions of salt often miss the mark. Therefore, I have not added salt to my recipes, unless it's on top of what is usually needed.

Where measurements of tins and trays are given, I understand that not all home cooks will own these exact items. You may need to adjust the cooking time and/or number of trays to make the recipes work well with the equipment you have.

Many people these days have food intolerances and allergies. I've included lists of recipes from the book that are gluten-, dairy- or egg-free. You will find them on page 250.

My hope is that these recipes will be as fun for you to make as they were for me to write. I have thoroughly enjoyed the process of putting this cookbook together and hope that the joy will flow on to you, as you cook from it, and on to those who get to enjoy the fruits of your labour. And don't forget the golden rule when cooking desserts and sweets ... you have to lick the bowl!

Introduction

My mum and dad laugh at the fact that I'm a foodie, as my relationship with food as a child was tenuous at best. I was one of those children who hated vegetables, ate only one type of fruit and one type of meat (sausage 'meat', of course!) and refused to try anything new. I have vivid memories of sitting at the dinner table wishing we had a dog who'd eat up the evidence of food I'd 'accidentally' dropped on the floor. And I have memories of my mum doing everything she could to interest me in a lunch box more adventurous than a Vegemite sandwich, an apple and a Poppa drink.

However, when it came to the world of sweet food, my attitude couldn't have been more different. I have memories of gathering crumbs off plates, licking bowls clean and always being aware of any sweet food hidden in the pantry. The rule in our household was that you had to finish all your meat and vegies before you had any dessert, and I think it's the only reason my body received the nutrition it needed!

Sweet food was my first love and to this day it is still where I feel most comfortable as a cook. Of course, I now enjoy eating just about every vegetable and meat known to man, but sweet food is unadulterated pleasure. Unlike the practical nature of food for fuel and nutrition, desserts are for no other purpose than to feel good. Endorphin food!

And the joy does not just come from eating it. There is so much more joy to be had when it is shared with others – to see the look of delight on my children's faces when they spot the freshly made chocolate cake; to experience a friend's 'Oh, I shouldn't' as they reach for the second warm cookie to have with their cup of tea; to see a sister take pleasure in the extra effort that's gone into a birthday dessert. The real driving force behind a love of cooking is so often a love of people.

My love of baking began as an eight-year-old during one of those long, hot summer holidays. I grew up in the era of cooking shows hosted by people like Peter Russell Clarke ('G'day!'), so after Mum suggested I cook something to relieve holiday boredom, I decided to put on my own TV cooking show. I measured out everything I needed for a coffee cake and began cooking it. It was the '80s when instant coffee reigned supreme, but coffee cake? Hours later, it turned out to be a gaudy, multi-layered cake, complete with piped icing decoration. But my dutiful family loved it, of course, and I remember it as the first time I created something that other people appreciated. I was hooked.

Throughout my schooling years I cooked intermittently. My sister, a friend and I would create 'restaurants' in the dining room. I convinced my friends that dress-up dinner parties were fun. I was even given the opportunity to cater for my uncle's work function. At the age of sixteen, when it came time to do the mandatory Year 10 work experience, I chose to do it in the commercial kitchen of a fine-dining restaurant. I loved that week, but I realised that if I did choose this industry I'd be working when everyone else was socialising and vice versa. As a sixteen-year-old with a social life to protect, this sounded terrible, and so I decided not to become a chef.

I chose instead to become a primary school teacher, and while I studied I worked as a waitress in an Italian family-run restaurant, observing the chef closely whenever I was in the kitchen. I learned so much from that family, not only about food, but also about how generosity and cooking with love translated into warm relationships. I began to see how food can be a wonderful tool for bringing people together.

I started to look for opportunities to cook for others: having friends over for dinner, cooking for church events, catering for extended-family functions, edible gifts of gratitude, even incorporating it into lessons I taught at school. My joy of cooking and fascination about food only deepened.

After the birth of our first child, Erin, I became a stay-at-home mum, and to this day it has been my most cherished work. I spent a lot of time baking and experimenting with recipes as Erin slept. When our second child, Liam, was born, life became much busier, but I still managed to bake a lot, often with little 'helpers' of my own usually appearing as bowls and spatulas required licking.

While I was pregnant with our third child, Maya, we made the big step of moving out of the city to Orange, the regional town in NSW we now call home. We knew before we moved that it was a foodie destination, but from the first week we arrived, when a large box of cherries landed on our doorstep, the way I cooked began to change. Rather than using my pantry stocks for inspiration, I began to use the produce that was so readily available. I scoured the local farmers' markets, visited local orchards to pick up the

freshest produce and, in time, even planted my own productive garden, with vegie patch, herb garden, fruit trees and chooks!

With so much literally on my doorstep I began experimenting more. It no longer seemed to matter so much if it didn't work as I could easily pick some more and try again! I still remained most confident in baking and any experimentation that didn't quite work out as planned was readily gobbled up by any family or friends who happened to be hovering. In fact, my friends began to expect that I would experiment on them – I still do – and I haven't heard any complaints yet!

As a busy mum with very young children I can't deny that some days cooking was simply about getting a meal on the table as quickly as I could, but on other days (or evenings when the kids were tucked up in bed) it was about finding my 'happy place'. It was a time to be in my own little world, enjoying the serenity of creativity … and the outcome of it! Cooking dishes like self-saucing chocolate puddings were almost an automatic reflex when I'd had a tough day. A batch of cookies often appeared when I was procrastinating or some sugar product eventuated if I was in the mood for learning.

Although I was gaining confidence to experiment, I was still a cook who relied heavily on recipes and other people's ideas when I entered *MasterChef Australia* 2011. I knew that I loved cooking, but I felt sure that I would last only a few weeks in the competition. However, I was keen to learn whatever I could from this once-in-a-lifetime experience, and take the opportunities offered to me for as long as they lasted. The books I read, conversations I had, food I tasted, cooking I observed and experiences I was immersed in afforded me a cooking learning curve like no other!

The recipes in this book are the culmination of that *MasterChef* experience. They represent the kind of cooking I love most: desserts and baked treats, including old favourites as well as new ideas. These recipes are also a marker of the cook

I am right now: still very much a home cook but one who has been on a wonderful journey of discovery. I've certainly learned a lot but cooking is one of life's pursuits in which you find that the more you know, the more you realise how little you know. But this excites me. It means that the journey of discovery will continue.

If I'm anything like my nanna, my journey will last well into my nineties! I have a few very precious hand-written recipes of hers. This makes me only too aware of how special it is that I have this opportunity to record mine in a book – a book that I can keep and pass on to my own children and grandchildren. And who knows … my great-grandchildren may even end up with a copy!

My hope, of course, is that these recipes will become ones you love too. That you will make them your own, and perhaps even pass them down your family line. After all, food may primarily be about nourishing the body, but when cooked with love for the people we love it becomes so much more than that. May your life be *The Sweet Life* too!

Kate Bracks, 2012

Syrups & sauces

The basics ...

Essentially a syrup is cooked sugar
and water. But when flavourings are
added, syrups become one of the
most versatile dessert techniques.
They can be served hot or cold, and
they are used in: sauces, sorbets,
jams, poaching liquids, meringues,
syrup cakes, pralines, nougat, glazes,
lollies, spun sugar ... and the list
goes on. Syrups can even be the main
element of a dessert if served with
fruit bobbing around in it!

Sauces, on the other hand, are always
an accompaniment, but they have the
potential to make an ordinary dessert
something really special.

Basic Sugar Syrup

Once you've mastered this technique, a whole new world of dessert-making will be opened up to you!

PREP TIME: *2 minutes*
COOKING TIME: *3–4 minutes*
MAKES: *180ml*

110G (½ CUP) CASTER SUGAR

125ML (½ CUP) WATER

1 Combine sugar and water in a small saucepan. Stir over medium-low heat, without boiling, until the sugar has dissolved.

2 Increase heat to medium and bring to the boil. Cook, without stirring, for 2 minutes.

3 Remove from the heat and use as required.

NOTE

This basic syrup can be made into a simple berry sauce. Add a punnet of berries to the hot syrup and leave to cool. Press through a sieve to remove any seeds. The syrup can also be infused with flavours such as ginger, lemongrass or cinnamon by placing the flavouring ingredient into the warm syrup and leaving it to cool to room temperature.

Caramel Syrup

Caramel syrup can be poured over ice cream, pancakes and fresh fruit, or can be used in cakes, crème caramels and ice creams.

PREP TIME: *2 minutes*
COOKING TIME: *10–15 minutes*
MAKES: *200ml*

220G (1 CUP) CASTER SUGAR

60ML (¼ CUP) WATER

80ML (⅓ CUP) HOT WATER, EXTRA

1 Combine the sugar with 60ml (¼ cup) of water in a small saucepan. Stir over low heat, without boiling, until all the sugar has dissolved.

2 Increase the heat to medium-high and bring to the boil. Brush down the sides of the pan with water, to ensure there are no sugar crystals on the side of the pan. Cook, without stirring, until the mixture reaches 165°C on a sugar thermometer or becomes light golden brown. This will take between 10 and 15 minutes, depending on your cooktop.

3 Remove from the heat and carefully add the 80ml (⅓ cup) hot water – beware, as it will react violently! Stir until smooth. If you find you have sugar crystal lumps, simply strain them off. Cool slightly and use as a liquid caramel.

NOTE

This can be made ahead of time and stored in a sealed container in the refrigerator. It may need heating slightly before use to get it back to its original consistency.

Chocolate Sauce

Everyone needs a good chocolate sauce recipe. Chocolate sauce goes with ice cream, cakes, waffles and puddings. Just remember the golden rule – the better quality chocolate you use, the better the flavour.

PREP TIME: *5 minutes*
COOKING TIME: *1–2 minutes*
MAKES: *250ml*

100G DARK CHOCOLATE, FINELY CHOPPED

50G MILK CHOCOLATE, FINELY CHOPPED

20G BUTTER

125ML (½ CUP) POURING CREAM

1 TSP VANILLA EXTRACT

1 Combine all the ingredients in a microwave-safe jug or bowl and microwave on high for 30 seconds. Stir and microwave again for a further 30 seconds. Repeat, if necessary, until all the chocolate is melted. Stir vigorously until the mixture comes together to a silky-smooth consistency.

2 Alternatively, you can combine all the ingredients in a heatproof bowl over a saucepan of simmering water (don't let the bottom of the bowl touch the water). When the chocolate is soft, remove from the heat and stir until smooth.

NOTE

You can also add things to a basic chocolate sauce to take it to a whole new level. Try infusing the cream with vanilla bean, star anise or cinnamon before melting the chocolate into it. Alternatively, you can stir through liqueurs such as Cognac, Kahlua or Cointreau.

Real Caramel Sauce

No other caramel sauce beats this one, in my opinion. It's a classic, creamy caramel and it's delicious!

PREP TIME: *2 minutes*
COOKING TIME: *10–15 minutes*
MAKES: *200ml*

220G (1 CUP) CASTER SUGAR

60ML (¼ CUP) WATER

160ML (⅔ CUP) POURING CREAM

1 Combine the sugar and water in a small saucepan. Stir over low heat, without boiling, until all the sugar has dissolved.

2 Increase the heat to medium-high and bring to the boil. Cook, without stirring, until the mixture reaches 165°C on a sugar thermometer or becomes light golden brown. This will take between 10 and 15 minutes, depending on your cooktop.

3 Meanwhile, in a separate saucepan, heat the cream until steaming.

4 Remove the syrup from the heat and carefully add the warm cream – beware, as it will react violently! Stir until the mixture is smooth. If you find you have sugar crystal lumps, simply strain them off. Cool slightly and use as required.

NOTE

This can be made ahead of time and stored in the fridge. It needs to be reheated slightly and stirred before use. It will keep for 7 days.

Simple Caramel Sauce

Technically, this is not a caramel, but it is what many of us associate with a caramel sauce. It's the kind you serve with sticky date pudding, or you could pour it over ice cream. It is so incredibly simple and tastes almost as good as the real thing.

PREP TIME: *5 minutes*
COOKING TIME: *5 minutes*
MAKES: *350ml*

110G (½ CUP) BROWN SUGAR

250ML (1 CUP) POURING CREAM

20G BUTTER

1 TSP VANILLA EXTRACT

1   Combine all the ingredients in a small saucepan over low heat. Stir occasionally until the butter is melted and the sugar is dissolved.

2   Increase the heat and simmer, stirring occasionally, for 5 minutes, or until the mixture is thick and syrupy.

Beyond the basics ...

Baked Honey and Rosemary Apples

Bees have given us ready-made syrup in honey. By heating it gently and adding one or two other ingredients, you have a very simple sauce. I was inspired by the combination of apple and rosemary when I cooked a Maggie Beer dish, so I've used that as my springboard for this recipe.

PREP TIME: *20 minutes*
COOKING TIME: *40 minutes*
MAKES: *4 serves*

230G (⅔ CUP) HONEY

1 TBS FINELY CHOPPED ROSEMARY

2 TSP WHITE WINE VINEGAR

PINCH OF SALT

4 SMALL-TO-MEDIUM PINK LADY APPLES

2 TBS CRÈME FRAÎCHE (SEE NOTE)

1 TBS FLAKED ALMONDS, TOASTED

4 SMALL SPRIGS ROSEMARY, TO GARNISH

1 Preheat the oven to 180°C. Lightly grease a baking dish large enough to hold the apples.

2 Combine the honey, rosemary, vinegar and salt in a small saucepan. Stir over low heat until the mixture is runny.

3 To prepare the apples, use an apple corer or small sharp knife to remove the apple cores. Peel the apples, and cut a thin slice from the base from each apple so they sit flat. Cut each apple crossways into 5–8mm slices. Keep them stacked so they maintain their original apple shape.

4 Dip each slice of apple into the syrup, and 'rebuild' the apple, slice by slice, into the prepared dish. Drizzle the remaining syrup over the apples and bake for 20 minutes. Baste with the pan juices and bake a further 20 minutes. Test for tenderness. If they aren't quite ready, baste again and cook for a further 5–10 minutes, until tender.

5 Drizzle the apples again with pan juices, and carefully lift each apple onto a serving plate. Spoon or pipe crème fraîche into the cavity of each apple. Scatter with toasted flaked almonds, and top with a rosemary sprig.

NOTE

Crème fraîche is a French-style sour cream but it is thicker and richer than most sour creams. It is found in the refrigerator section of your supermarket. This dish would also work well using pears.

Tropical Fruit Salad with Lemongrass Syrup

At the height of summer when tropical fruits are at their best, there is little that is more refreshing and satisfying than a humble fruit salad. Try this version with a simple lemongrass syrup, which ties all the flavours together.

PREP TIME: *25 minutes*
COOKING TIME: *2–3 minutes + standing*
MAKES: *4 serves*

75G (⅓ CUP) CASTER SUGAR

80ML (⅓ CUP) WATER

1 STICK LEMONGRASS, TRIMMED, BRUISED

JUICE OF ½ A LIME

½ SWEET, RIPE PINEAPPLE

2 RIPE MANGOES

2 PASSIONFRUIT

5 MINT LEAVES, FINELY SHREDDED

MANGO SORBET, TO SERVE (SEE PAGE 143)

1   To make the lemongrass syrup, combine the sugar and water in a small saucepan. Stir over medium-low heat, without boiling, until the sugar has dissolved. Add the lemongrass to the hot syrup and bring to a simmer. Cook without stirring for 2–3 minutes. Remove from the heat and set aside for 10–15 minutes, for the flavour to infuse. Strain to remove the lemongrass, and add the lime juice.

2   To prepare the fruit, cut the skin, eyes and core from the pineapple, and slice thinly. Cut each slice into pieces roughly triangular in shape. Peel and stone the mangoes, and cut into pieces. Halve the passionfruit and scoop out the pulp, discarding the skins.

3   Arrange the fruit into serving bowls and drizzle with passionfruit pulp. Pour a little lemongrass syrup onto each, sprinkle with mint and finish with a scoop of mango sorbet.

NOTE

The syrup can be made ahead of time and stored in an airtight container. The fruit salad is best prepared just prior to serving. You can use any tropical fruits you like. For something a bit different, try including pawpaw, star fruit, lychee, mangosteen or rambutan.

Crumbly Caramel Peaches and Cream

This is one of those recipes where elements of the recipe could be used as an accompaniment to other dishes. For example, the caramel peaches would work well with a flourless almond cake, or the macadamia crumble would work well accompanying pieces of poached pears.

PREP TIME: *25 minutes*
COOKING TIME: *about 25 minutes*
MAKES: *4 serves*

CARAMEL PEACHES

4 RIPE PEACHES

220G (1 CUP) CASTER SUGAR

100ML WATER

80ML HOT WATER, EXTRA

MACADAMIA CRUMBLE

75G (½ CUP) PLAIN FLOUR

55G (¼ CUP) BROWN SUGAR

PINCH OF SALT

60G BUTTER, CUBED

60G (½ CUP) MACADAMIAS, ROUGHLY CHOPPED

125ML THICK DOUBLE CREAM, TO SERVE

1 To prepare the peaches, score a small cross in the skin on the base of each peach, and place into a heatproof bowl. Cover with boiling water, and stand for 1 minute. Drain, and when cool enough to handle, slip off the skins. Cut into 1cm wedges, and discard the stones. Place the peaches into a heatproof bowl.

2 For the caramel peaches, combine the sugar and 100ml water in a small saucepan. Stir over medium-low heat until all the sugar has dissolved. Increase the heat to medium-high and bring to the boil. Cook, without stirring, until the mixture reaches 165°C on a sugar thermometer or becomes light golden brown. This will take between 10 and 15 minutes, depending on your cooktop. Carefully add the extra hot water to the pan – take care, as it will spit and splutter! (If you have sugar crystals at this point, don't despair. Return it to the heat and stir occasionally until they disappear or reduce in size. Strain the liquid and no one will know the difference!) Pour the syrup over the peaches and leave to cool.

3 To make the crumble, preheat the oven to 180°C and line a baking tray with baking paper. Combine the flour and sugar in a bowl with the pinch of salt. Add the butter cubes and rub the mixture between your fingers until it is incorporated well and looks crumbly (I personally like big chunky bits in mine). Add the macadamias and spread onto the prepared tray. Bake for 15–20 minutes, or until it's golden and 'crumbly'. Allow it to cool then crumble lightly with your hands.

4 Pile the peaches into individual serving bowls or glasses. Spoon a little of the caramel over, and top with the crumble mixture. Serve with a dollop of cream.

NOTE

Caramel peaches and crumble can be made ahead of time and stored separately in airtight containers, ready to assemble just before serving. You could easily use the same process with a different fruit. Try nectarines, plums, mixed berries or even banana!

Strawberries in Dessert Wine Syrup with Crushed Amaretti

This is one of the simplest desserts to make, and yet it's delicious. As a dessert on its own it is light and refreshing, or for more decadence it could be served as an accompaniment to a cake or panna cotta.

PREP TIME: *15 minutes*
COOKING TIME: *5 minutes + cooling*
MAKES: *4 serves*

DESSERT WINE SYRUP

110G (½ CUP) CASTER SUGAR

300ML DESSERT WINE

1 VANILLA BEAN, SPLIT,
SEEDS SCRAPED

500G STRAWBERRIES, HULLED

JUICE OF ½ A LIME

4 AMARETTI BISCUITS

SMALL MINT LEAVES, TO SERVE

1 To make the dessert wine syrup, combine the sugar and dessert wine in a small saucepan over low heat and stir without boiling until the sugar has dissolved. Add the vanilla bean and bring to a simmer. Simmer gently for 5 minutes.

2 To prepare the strawberries, cut them into quarters and place into a heatproof bowl.

3 Tip the warm syrup onto the strawberries and add the lime juice, stirring to combine. Set aside to cool to room temperature.

4 Serve the strawberries in glasses, with 2–3 dessert spoons of syrup in each glass. Sprinkle with crushed amaretti biscuits, and top with mint leaves.

NOTE

This can be made ahead of time and left covered at room temperature.

Homemade Honeycomb with Grand Marnier Chocolate Dipping Sauce

Combine your syrup-making and sauce-making skills to create this special treat. It's delicious as a stand-alone dessert, or could form part of a fondue spread, or even jazz up a simple chocolate cake.

PREP TIME: *20 minutes*
COOKING TIME: *10-15 minutes*
MAKES: *4 serves*

HONEYCOMB

165G (¾ CUP) CASTER SUGAR

1 ½ TBS HONEY

¼ CUP (60ML) GLUCOSE SYRUP (SEE NOTE)

2 TBS WATER

2 TSP BI-CARB SODA

GRAND MARNIER CHOCOLATE DIPPING SAUCE

100G DARK CHOCOLATE, FINELY CHOPPED

50G MILK CHOCOLATE, FINELY CHOPPED

20G BUTTER

125ML (½ CUP) POURING CREAM

1 TSP VANILLA EXTRACT

2–3 TSP GRAND MARNIER

1   For the honeycomb, line a large baking tray (at least 25cm x 20cm and about 1–2cm deep) with baking paper. Keep it close to your cooktop. Combine the caster sugar, honey, glucose and water in a medium-large saucepan. Stir over low heat, without boiling, until the sugar has dissolved. Increase the heat to medium-high and bring to a gentle boil. Cook, without stirring, until the mixture reaches 165°C on a sugar thermometer or becomes light golden brown. This will take between 10 and 15 minutes, depending on your cooktop – don't let it get too brown or it will be bitter. Stir in the bi-carb soda, being aware that it will foam up vigorously. As soon as it is very foamy, pour it into the baking tray. Set aside for about 15 minutes, to cool and harden.

2   To make the chocolate dipping sauce, combine all the ingredients except the Grand Marnier in a microwave-safe jug or bowl. Microwave on high for 30 seconds. Stir and microwave again for a further 30 seconds. Repeat, if necessary, until the chocolate has melted. Stir vigorously until smooth and glossy. Add Grand Marnier to taste. Leave to cool and thicken slightly.

3   To serve, spoon the chocolate sauce into serving bowls or jugs. Cut or break the honeycomb into large shards and serve with the sauce for dipping.

NOTE

Both the honeycomb and the sauce can be made ahead of time and stored separately in airtight containers until ready to assemble and serve. The chocolate sauce will need to be refrigerated and then warmed again when ready to serve. Glucose syrup is available in the baking section of most supermarkets. For another delicious dessert, stir left-over honeycomb and chocolate sauce through softened vanilla ice cream and then re-freeze it.

Vincotto Figs with Caramelised Walnuts and Mascarpone

I never really liked figs until a friend made me a fig pizza with caramelised onion and goat's cheese. I couldn't get enough of it! The combination of figs with caramel and soft cheese is impossible for me to resist. Here's a dessert version of a similar flavour combination. If fresh figs are not in season, this recipe also works well with ripe pears.

PREP TIME: *20 minutes*
COOKING TIME: *about 20 minutes + cooling*
MAKES: *4 serves*

VINCOTTO FIGS

110G (½ CUP) CASTER SUGAR

125ML (½ CUP) WATER

50ML VINCOTTO (SEE NOTE)

8 RIPE FIGS

CARAMELISED WALNUTS

220G (1 CUP) CASTER SUGAR

180ML (¾ CUP) WATER

60G (⅔ CUP) WALNUTS

SWEET MASCARPONE

180G (¾ CUP) MASCARPONE

1 TBS ICING SUGAR, SIFTED

1 For the vincotto figs, combine the sugar and water in a small saucepan. Stir over medium-low heat until the sugar has dissolved. Stir in the vincotto and increase the heat to bring to a simmer. Cook, without stirring, for 5–8 minutes, or until it is a syrupy consistency.

2 To prepare the figs, cut each one into quarters, without going right through the base. Pinch each fig at its base to help it open up. Place snugly into a deep, heatproof dish and pour the syrup over the figs. Leave figs to sit in the syrup while you prepare the walnuts.

3 For the caramelised walnuts, combine the sugar and water in a small saucepan and stir over low heat until the sugar has dissolved. Increase the heat and bring to a simmer. Cook, without stirring, for 10–15 minutes, or until it becomes a medium brown colour.

4 Meanwhile, toast the walnuts in a dry frying pan over medium-low heat until they have taken on a little colour and become fragrant. Line a baking tray with baking paper. When the syrup has reached its desired colour, add the walnuts to the syrup then spoon them out individually onto the baking paper. Leave for about 10 minutes, until they cool and harden.

5 For the sweet mascarpone, place the ingredients into a bowl and stir until thoroughly combined.

6 To serve, place two figs onto each serving plate. Top each with a dollop of sweet mascarpone and drizzle with the vincotto syrup. Scatter walnuts on and around the figs.

NOTE

Each component can be prepared ahead of time and assembled just before serving. Vincotto (also known as vino cotto) is a condiment made from grape must. It can be likened to caramelised balsamic vinegar (but it is not actually a vinegar), so use this if you cannot get vincotto. These caramelised walnuts can be used in so many dishes, both sweet and savoury. Try them on ice cream sundaes, with chocolate cakes or on cheese platters.

Peanut and Salted Caramel Sundae

It wasn't all that long ago that I was introduced to salted caramel. From my first mouthful I was a convert. That sweet, salty combination is unusual in dessert but oh-so-fantastic! But if the idea really doesn't appeal to you, just leave the salt out.

PREP TIME: *20 minutes*
COOKING TIME: *15 minutes*
MAKES: *4 serves*

295G (1⅓ CUPS) CASTER SUGAR

200ML WATER

100ML POURING CREAM

70G (½ CUP) UNSALTED PEANUTS

1 TSP SEA SALT FLAKES

GOOD-QUALITY VANILLA ICE CREAM, TO SERVE (SEE PAGE 88)

1 To make the caramel, combine the sugar and water in a small saucepan. Stir over low heat, without boiling, until the sugar has dissolved. Increase the heat to medium-high and bring to the boil. Cook, without stirring, until the mixture reaches 165°C on a sugar thermometer or becomes light golden brown. This will take between 10 and 15 minutes, depending on your cooktop.

2 Place the cream into a small saucepan and warm over medium-low heat until steaming. Keep warm without boiling until ready to use.

3 Meanwhile, place the peanuts into a dry frying pan over low heat. Cook, shaking the pan regularly, until coloured and fragrant. Place onto a baking paper-lined tray, keeping them close together (roughly within a 12cm x 12cm square).

4 To make the praline, pour about half the caramel over the peanuts. Set aside for 15–20 minutes, to cool and harden.

5 For the caramel sauce you need to work quickly. Add the hot cream to the remaining caramel, being very careful as it will react violently! Stir over low heat until smooth. Stir in the salt flakes.

6 To serve, roughly chop the peanut praline. Place 2 scoops of ice cream into serving bowls. Drizzle with caramel sauce and scatter with the peanut praline.

NOTE

Each component can be made ahead of time and assembled just prior to serving. If the process of making traditional caramel sauce scares you, another alternative is to serve up vanilla ice cream with the Simple Caramel Sauce (page 21) and scatter it with chopped macadamia – it won't quite be the same but it will still be delicious!

The basics…

French Meringue

Swiss Meringue

Italian Meringue

Beyond the basics…

Balsamic Pavlova with Strawberry Cream

Orange Blossom and
Pistachio Meringues

Chocolate, Date and Hazelnut Torte

Passionfruit Meringue Roll

Little Lime Meringue Pies

Little Chocolate Meringues

Meringue

The basics...

Meringue is such a versatile dessert technique. It can simply be caramelised on the outside for a rich and creamy texture on the inside, it can be partially baked to create a chewy fudgy texture, or it can be cooked right through to result in a powdery crunch. It can have other ingredients stirred through it, piled on top of it or nestled underneath it. There is so much scope to be creative when cooking with meringue!

There are three basic ways of making meringue. French meringue is the simplest as it requires no heating. However, if you are willing to go to a bit more effort, you'll reap the rewards because Swiss and Italian meringues produce a thicker, glossier end result with a texture that is so much finer on the palate than the French meringue.

Tips for meringue-making success:

- Using an electric mixer certainly makes the job of making meringue much easier, but if you don't have one, a bowl, whisk and lots of arm action will get you good results too!

- Ensure the bowl and whisk attachments of your electric mixer are perfectly clean. The tiniest amount of fat or oil will mean that your meringue won't work.

- When separating the eggs into whites and yolks, you must ensure there is no egg yolk in the whites as this has a fat content that will mean your meringue won't work. I break one egg at a time into two glasses (one for whites and one for yolks) then tip each white into the bowl separately to make sure I don't waste lots of egg if I get yolk into one.

- When you rub the beaten meringue mixture between your thumb and finger you should not feel any sugar granules – they should have dissolved. If they haven't, keep whisking until you can no longer feel them. If they do not dissolve they can cause your meringue to weep and crystallise on its surface.

French Meringue

6 EGG WHITES

PINCH OF SALT

330G (1½ CUPS) CASTER SUGAR

1　Place the egg whites, salt and a couple of spoonfuls of the sugar into a large bowl.

2　Whisk the egg whites at medium speed until they begin to foam. Increase the speed to high and whisk for 1–2 minutes, until the mixture turns white and forms soft, smooth peaks when you dip a finger in.

3　Reduce the speed to medium, and gradually add the remaining sugar a spoonful at a time until it's all incorporated.

4　Scrape down the sides of the bowl then increase the speed to high again for five minutes or until the meringue looks glossy, holds its shape when you lift the beaters and is without any gritty sugar feel.

5　Now it's ready to use in another application.

Swiss Meringue

6 EGG WHITES

PINCH OF SALT

330G (1½ CUPS) CASTER SUGAR

1　Place the egg whites, salt and sugar into a large heatproof bowl that fits snugly over a saucepan of simmering water. Make sure the bottom of the bowl does not touch the water.

2　Using electric hand beaters, whisk the mixture constantly until it becomes the temperature of very hot water. If you have a thermometer it should reach 65°C. If you don't have a thermometer it's the temperature where you can dip your finger in but you wouldn't want to leave it there! It will look the consistency of frothy milk.

3　Tip the hot mixture into the large bowl of an electric stand mixer and whisk on high until it stops steaming. Reduce the speed to medium and whisk until the mixture is just warm. Reduce the speed to low and whisk until the mixture is room temperature.

4　Now it's ready to use in another application.

Italian Meringue

220G (1 CUP) CASTER SUGAR

110ML WATER

4 EGG WHITES

PINCH OF SALT

1　Put the sugar and water into a heavy-based saucepan and stir over low heat without boiling until the sugar has dissolved.

2　Increase the heat and bring to the boil. Cook for 7–8 minutes, or until it reaches 128°C on a sugar thermometer. If you don't have a sugar thermometer, spoon a little bit into some cold water. It should cool to form a firm ball when pinched between your fingertips. If it doesn't, continue cooking the syrup and then test again.

3　Put the egg whites and salt into the large bowl of an electric mixer and whisk on low speed until the mixture foams. With the beaters still running, gradually trickle in the syrup as soon as it has reached the required temperature, ensuring it doesn't splash all over the bowl!

4　Continue whisking for 5–10 minutes, until the mixture comes back to room temperature.

5　Now it's ready to use in another application.

Beyond the basics ...

Balsamic Pavlova with Strawberry Cream

When I cooked René Redzepi's famous 'Snowman', the meringue base was a vinegar meringue and I loved its extra zing! Knowing that strawberries and balsamic vinegar make a wonderful pair, I decided to put the two together to create a pavlova ... and I love the end result!

PREP TIME: *30 minutes*
COOKING TIME: *1 hour
 + cooling in the oven*
MAKES: *10–12 slices pavlova*

MERINGUE

6 EGG WHITES

PINCH OF SALT

330G (1½ CUPS) CASTER SUGAR

80ML (⅓ CUP) BALSAMIC VINEGAR

1 TBS CORNFLOUR

55G (⅓ CUP) ICING SUGAR, SIFTED

STRAWBERRY CREAM

2 PUNNETS STRAWBERRIES

1 TBS ICING SUGAR, SIFTED

250ML (1 CUP) POURING CREAM

1 TSP VANILLA EXTRACT

1 Preheat the oven to 150°C. Use a pencil to draw a 20cm round onto a sheet of baking paper (trace around a plate). Grease a baking tray, and place the paper onto it, pencil-side down.

2 To make the meringue, place the egg whites, salt and a couple of spoonfuls of the sugar into the bowl. Begin whisking the egg white at medium speed until it begins to foam. Increase the speed to high and whisk for 1–2 minutes, until it turns white and forms soft, smooth peaks when you dip a finger in. With the mixer running on medium speed, gradually add the remaining sugar a spoonful at a time until it's all incorporated.

3 Scrape down the sides of the bowl then increase the speed to high again for 5 minutes, or until the meringue looks glossy, holds its shape when you lift the beaters and is without any gritty sugar feel.

4 Reduce the speed to low. Add the balsamic vinegar and mix well, scraping down the sides of the bowl as necessary. Sift the cornflour and icing sugar over the mixture and whisk again until incorporated.

5 Using a spatula, pile the mixture onto the baking tray inside the drawn circle. Keep it tall initially, then spread it evenly to the edges, creating a cake shape.

6 Place into the oven. Immediately reduce the oven temperature to 140°C and bake for 1 hour. Turn the oven off but leave the pavlova in there until it has cooled to room temperature. Don't worry too much if it cracks as it will be smothered in strawberry cream!

7 Meanwhile, to make the strawberry cream, hull 1 punnet of the strawberries and cut them into 1cm pieces. Place into a bowl, sprinkle over the icing sugar and stir to coat. Set aside for 15 minutes.

8 Whip the cream and vanilla to soft peaks. Stir through the chopped strawberries and up to 1 teaspoon of any liquid from them.

9 Quarter the remaining strawberries. Spread the strawberry cream on top of the pavlova and scatter with the quartered strawberries.

NOTE

Using pure icing sugar keeps this recipe gluten-free.

Orange Blossom and Pistachio Meringues

I love Middle Eastern flavours, especially those used in desserts. Here, I've chosen the classic combination of orange blossom and pistachio to combine with the familiar textures of chewy meringue and luxurious cream.

PREP TIME: *20 minutes*
COOKING TIME: *45 minutes*
 + 2 hours cooling
MAKES: *8 serves*

MERINGUE

6 EGG WHITES

PINCH OF SALT

110G (½ CUP) CASTER SUGAR

110G (⅔ CUP) ICING SUGAR,
SIFTED

1 TBS CORNFLOUR

1 TSP ORANGE BLOSSOM WATER

30G (¼ CUP) BLANCHED
PISTACHIOS, FINELY CHOPPED
(SEE NOTE)

ORANGE BLOSSOM CREAM

200ML POURING CREAM

½ TSP ORANGE BLOSSOM WATER,
EXTRA

6 SMALL ORANGES
(OR 3 LARGE ONES)

2 TBS BLANCHED PISTACHIOS,
EXTRA

1 Preheat the oven to 140°C. Grease a large baking tray and line with baking paper.

2 To make the meringues, place the egg whites and a pinch of salt into the bowl of an electric mixer with the whisk attachment. Whisk on high speed until firm peaks form (3–4 minutes). With the motor running on medium speed, spoon the caster sugar in, one spoonful at a time. Once it has all been added, increase the speed to high again and whisk for a further 2–3 minutes. Sift the icing sugar and cornflour over the mixture and mix to combine thoroughly. Fold in the orange blossom water and the finely chopped pistachios. Taste to check, as different brands of orange blossom water are different strengths. It needs to taste lightly fragrant – you may need to add more.

3 Spoon 8 mounds of meringue onto the prepared baking tray, spreading gently with the back of a spoon to make 8cm rounds. Leave room between them for spreading. Bake for 45 minutes, or until the meringues have set on the outside and lift from the oven tray. Remove them from the oven and set aside to cool completely.

4 Whisk the cream to soft peaks. Add the extra orange blossom water and mix thoroughly. Taste to check the flavour of the orange blossom water and add more if needed.

5   To segment the oranges, cut the tops and bases off them. Standing them on their base, use a small, sharp knife to cut down around the curve of the orange, removing the orange skin and the white pith. Try not to leave any pith as it is bitter and unpleasant to eat. Looking at the peeled orange you will see its natural segments. Run your knife down each side of each membrane, stopping at the centre. The orange segments should basically fall away. This is the pot of gold at the end of the rainbow!

6   To serve, place a meringue on each serving plate. Top with orange blossom cream, orange segments and sprinkle with blanched pistachios.

NOTE

The meringues can be made ahead of time and kept in an airtight container. Assemble just prior to serving. Blanched pistachios are available from specialty food shops. Using pure icing sugar keeps this recipe gluten-free.

Chocolate, Date and Hazelnut Torte

This is a simple and delicious dessert, but be warned … it's rich! You'll need others around you to help you indulge in this one (and, yes – for those of you who watched it being cooked on MasterChef, yours will have 3 layers!).

PREP TIME: *40 minutes*
COOKING TIME: *45 minutes*
MAKES: *10–12 slices*

TORTE LAYERS

6 EGG WHITES

PINCH OF SALT

330G (1½ CUPS) CASTER SUGAR

300G (2 CUPS) PITTED DATES, CHOPPED

300G HAZELNUTS, CHOPPED (SEE NOTE)

300G DARK CHOCOLATE, CHOPPED

MASCARPONE FILLING

250ML (1 CUP) THICKENED CREAM

250G (1 CUP) MASCARPONE

2 TBS ICING SUGAR, SIFTED

1 TBS COINTREAU

CHOCOLATE GLAZE

75G GOOD-QUALITY DARK CHOCOLATE, CHOPPED

25G GOOD-QUALITY MILK CHOCOLATE, CHOPPED

80ML (⅓ CUP) THICKENED CREAM

20G BUTTER

1   Preheat the oven to 160°C. Use a pencil to draw a 17cm round onto each of 3 sheets of baking paper (trace around a plate). Grease 3 baking trays (large enough to leave room for spreading), and place the paper onto them, pencil-side down. This will be your guide for spreading the torte mixture.

2   To make the meringue base for the torte layers, place the egg whites, salt and a couple of spoonfuls of the sugar into the bowl of an electric mixer. Whisk the egg white at medium speed until it begins to foam. Increase the speed to high and whisk for 1–2 minutes, until it turns white and forms soft, smooth peaks when you dip a finger in. Reduce the speed to medium, and gradually add the remaining sugar a spoonful at a time until it's all incorporated. Scrape down the sides of the bowl then increase the speed to high again for 5 minutes, or until the meringue looks glossy, holds its shape when you lift the beaters and is without any gritty sugar feel.

3   For the torte layers, fold the chopped dates, hazelnuts and chocolate through the meringue until evenly incorporated. Spread ⅓ of the mixture onto each of the baking trays, using the traced circles as a guide. Keep them an even thickness. Bake for 45 minutes or until the surface is firm and lightly golden. Leave them to cool on the trays until ready to assemble.

4   To make the mascarpone filling, beat the thickened cream and mascarpone until soft peaks form. Sift in the icing sugar and pour in the Cointreau. Beat until smooth and stiff peaks are formed in the cream.

5   To make the chocolate glaze, combine the chocolate, cream and butter in a bowl over a pan of simmering water (don't let the bottom of the bowl touch the water). Stir until the chocolate and butter are melted and the mixture is smooth. Remove the bowl from the saucepan and cool slightly.

6   To assemble the torte, place one meringue layer onto a serving plate. Spread with half the mascarpone filling. Place a second layer on top and spread on the remaining mascarpone filling. Top with the final layer and drizzle over the chocolate glaze.

NOTE

Each component can be made ahead of time. Store filling and glaze in the fridge and then gently re-warm the glaze before pouring it on. Use pure icing sugar to keep this recipe gluten-free.

Passionfruit Meringue Roll

This recipe is really a pavlova in a more sophisticated form. In my opinion, a traditional pavlova is never complete without a little passionfruit, but here I've made it the undeniable star!

PREP TIME: *30 minutes*
COOKING TIME: *12 minutes*
 + 2 hours setting
MAKES: *6 slices*

PASSIONFRUIT SYRUP

180ML (¾ CUP) PASSIONFRUIT JUICE (SEE NOTE)

75G (⅓ CUP) CASTER SUGAR

MERINGUE

6 EGG WHITES

PINCH OF SALT

330G (1½ CUPS) CASTER SUGAR

1 TBS CORNFLOUR

2 TBS CASTER SUGAR, EXTRA

FILLING

160G (⅔ CUP) MASCARPONE

160ML (⅔ CUP) POURING CREAM

1 TBS ICING SUGAR, SIFTED

ICING SUGAR, EXTRA, TO DUST

1   Preheat oven to 160°C. Grease a baking tray (38cm x 25cm x 2cm deep) and line with baking paper, allowing it to hang over the edges by about 5cm.

2   Place the passionfruit juice and sugar into a small saucepan and stir over low heat until the sugar has dissolved. Increase the heat and bring to a simmer. Cook for about 4 minutes, or until the mixture is slightly syrupy. Remove from the heat and set aside to cool.

3   Make a French meringue according to the method on page 42. Sift the cornflour onto the mixture and whisk for 30 seconds to incorporate.

4   Spread the meringue evenly over the prepared tray. Bake for 12 minutes, until the meringue has just formed a skin. Remove it from the oven and leave it to cool for 5 minutes.

5   Place a 40cm-length of baking paper onto a large chopping board and sprinkle with the extra caster sugar. Carefully turn the warm, cooked meringue out onto this paper and allow it to cool.

6   For the filling, whisk the mascarpone and cream until soft peaks form. Stir through the icing sugar, then fold through ⅔ of the cooled passionfruit syrup.

7   Spread the passionfruit cream onto the cooled meringue, leaving a 1cm border on all sides. Starting from a short end, and using the baking paper to help you manoeuvre it, carefully roll up the meringue, Swiss roll style. Wrap the baking paper firmly around the roll to secure it and place seam-side down onto a tray. Refrigerate for at least 2 hours.

8   Remove the baking paper from the roll and trim the ends. Dust with sifted icing sugar. Cut into 6 thick slices and place onto serving plates. Drizzle with the remaining passionfruit syrup.

NOTE

This recipe is best eaten on the day it's baked, but it does need a couple of hours in the fridge to set. To create ¾ cup passionfruit juice, place the pulp from 18 passionfruit into the bowl of a hand-held stick blender. Blend until runny. Pour through a sieve to remove the seeds. Stir ½ teaspoon of seeds back into the juice. Top up with orange juice if necessary. Using pure icing sugar keeps this recipe gluten-free.

Little Lime Meringue Pies

My dad has always loved Lemon Meringue Pie, in particular his recipe with a biscuit base and creamy centre. Here, I've given an old-fashioned lemon meringue pie a contemporary little twist. Hopefully he'll love these ones just as much!

PREP TIME: *40 minutes*
COOKING TIME: *10 minutes + 1 hour setting*
MAKES: *12*

BISCUIT BASE

125G SCOTCH FINGER BISCUITS, BROKEN UP

50G BUTTER, MELTED

FILLING

395G CAN CONDENSED MILK

2 EGG YOLKS

FINELY GRATED ZEST OF 1 LIME

125ML (½ CUP) LIME JUICE (ABOUT 3 LIMES)

MERINGUE

2 EGG WHITES

PINCH OF SALT

110G (½ CUP) CASTER SUGAR

1 Grease 12 patty cake tins. For the biscuit base, place the biscuits into a food processor and process to fine crumbs. Tip into a bowl and stir through the melted butter. The mixture should hold together when pushed with the back of a spoon. If it's still too crumbly to do that add a little extra melted butter. Divide the crumb mixture evenly among the holes of the tin and press down with your fingers to create a firm base. Refrigerate while you prepare the filling.

2 For the filling, combine the condensed milk, egg yolks, zest and juice in a bowl and mix to combine thoroughly. Spoon onto the biscuit bases.

3 Preheat the oven to 180°C.

4 To make the meringue, place the egg whites, salt and a couple of spoonfuls of the sugar into the bowl of an electric mixer. Whisk the egg white at medium speed until it begins to foam. Increase the speed to high and whisk for 1–2 minutes, until the mixture turns white and forms soft, smooth peaks when you dip a finger in. Reduce the speed to medium, and gradually add the remaining sugar a spoonful at a time until it's all incorporated. Scrape down the sides of the bowl then increase the speed to high again for 5 minutes, or until the meringue looks glossy, holds its shape when you lift the beaters and is without any gritty sugar feel.

5 Spoon or pipe the meringue onto the filling, leaving a 5mm gap around the edge. Bake for 10 minutes or until lightly golden. Allow the pies to come back to room temperature and then refrigerate for 30 minutes (until the base and filling are set).

6 Run a sharp knife around the edge of each little pie and lift out. If the base does not lift easily, refrigerate for a little longer and then try again. Be careful though – if these little pies are kept in the fridge too long the meringue begins to sweat.

NOTE

The base and filling can be made ahead of time and kept in the refrigerator. The meringue should be done no more than 2 hours before serving.

Little Chocolate Meringues

These little meringues make a great treat to have with coffee after a meal, or to take to a friend's house if they're cooking for you. They are the perfect way to use up egg whites that are often left over from other recipes.

PREP TIME: *30 minutes*

COOKING TIME: *10 minutes*

MAKES: *12–15*

MERINGUES

3 EGG WHITES

PINCH OF SALT

165G (¾ CUP) CASTER SUGAR

2 TSP COCOA POWDER

CHOCOLATE COATING

80G COUVERTURE MILK CHOCOLATE (SEE NOTE)

1 Preheat the oven to 120°C. Grease a large baking tray and line with baking paper.

2 To make the meringue, place the egg whites, salt and sugar into a large bowl that fits tightly above a saucepan of simmering water (make sure the bottom of the bowl does not touch the water).

3 Whisk the mixture constantly until it becomes the temperature of very hot water. If you have a thermometer it should reach 65°C. If you don't have a thermometer it's the temperature where you can dip your finger in but you wouldn't want to leave it there! It will look the consistency of frothy milk.

4 Tip the hot mixture into the large bowl of an electric mixer and whisk on high until it stops steaming. Reduce the speed to medium and whisk until the mixture is just warm. Reduce the speed to low and whisk until the mixture is room temperature. Sift over the cocoa powder and mix through thoroughly.

5 Spoon the mixture into a piping bag fitted with a 1cm fluted star nozzle and pipe 12–15 star-shaped meringues onto the prepared tray. Bake for 10 minutes and then turn the oven off. Leave the meringues in the oven until cooled to room temperature.

6 Line another tray with baking paper. Melt the chocolate and dip the base of each cooled meringue into the chocolate. Place onto the tray and leave for 30 minutes until set.

NOTE

Couverture chocolate is very good-quality chocolate, which sets beautifully. It is available from specialty food shops. Use any good-quality milk chocolate if you can't find it. For a different flavour, substitute the cocoa for 1 teaspoon of vanilla extract and dip the cooked meringues in white chocolate.

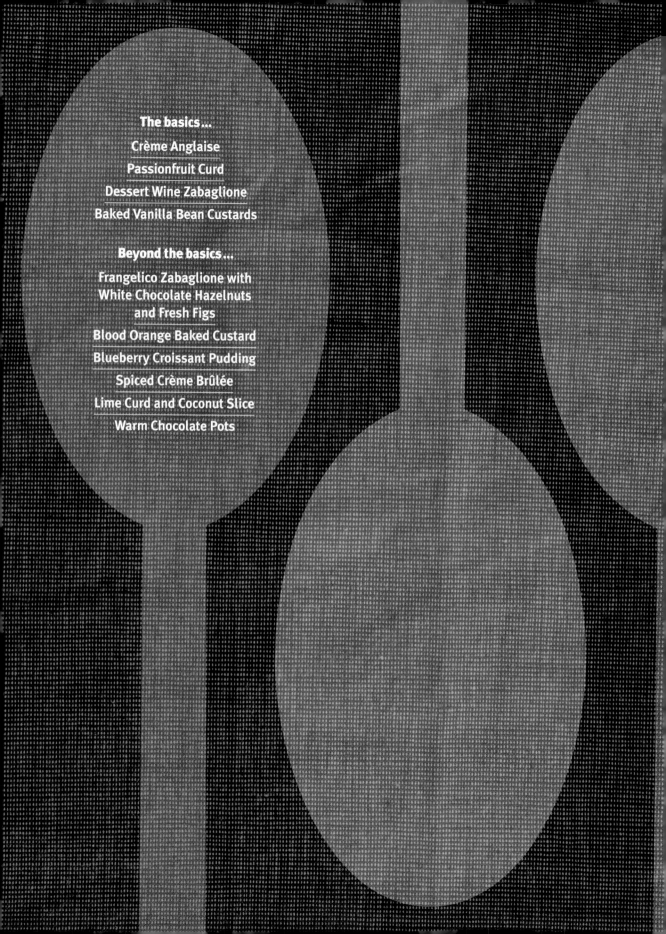

Custards
& sabayons

The basics...

A custard is a hot or cold mixture
thickened or set with eggs or egg
yolks. Custards often contain milks
or creams, but not always. The world
of custards is an enormous one so
I've selected a few I think will be
useful in any kitchen. I've included in
this chapter pouring custards, baked
custards, zabaglione (or sabayon)
and curds.

Custards are such a wonderful
base for sauces, ice creams,
puddings, fillings and toppings,
as they can take on a multitude of
flavour profiles. They can also be
the star component of a dessert,
or take the supporting role of an
accompaniment. Either way, they are
indispensable in the dessert kitchen.

Crème Anglaise

Crème Anglaise forms the basis of so many desserts, as well as being a beautiful accompaniment to a wide range of other desserts. I have even been known to sit down with a bowl of it and nothing else! Its name is French for 'English cream', but it simply means a thin custard. Everything sounds better in French though, doesn't it?

PREP TIME: *10 minutes*
COOKING TIME: *5–10 minutes*
MAKES: *700ml*

250ML (1 CUP) MILK

250ML (1 CUP) POURING CREAM

1 VANILLA BEAN, SPLIT,
SEEDS SCRAPED

5 EGG YOLKS

110G (½ CUP) CASTER SUGAR

1 Combine the milk, cream, vanilla bean and seeds in a medium saucepan. Place over medium heat and heat until steaming.

2 Meanwhile, whisk the egg yolks and sugar together in a bowl until thick and pale.

3 Gradually pour the milk mixture into the egg mixture, whisking constantly.

4 Rinse out the saucepan to remove any milk sediment. Pour the mixture back into the saucepan through a sieve, to remove the vanilla pod and any lumps that may have formed.

5 Cook over medium heat, stirring constantly with a soft spatula, until the mixture coats the back of a spoon (when you swipe your finger across the spoon, the liquid holds and does not drip down through the swipe). It takes 5–10 minutes depending on your stove. Take care not to boil, or the mixture will curdle. Remove from the heat.

6 If storing for later use, pour into a container and cover the surface directly with plastic wrap to stop a skin forming. When ready to serve, remove the plastic wrap and gently reheat.

NOTE

It is easy to add a different flavour dimension to Crème Anglaise. At the end of cooking, add 30ml of a liqueur such as brandy, Grand Marnier, Kahlua or Frangelico. Alternatively, infuse the milk and cream mixture before you add it to the eggs. Try infusing with chopped ginger, orange zest or cinnamon quills.

Passionfruit Curd

A curd is a basic custard mixture that has been flavoured with fruit, usually citrus. It is delicious slathered onto hot toast or used as a filling for cakes or tarts.

PREP TIME: *5 minutes*

COOKING TIME: *10 minutes + 1 hour chilling*

MAKES: *250ml (1 cup)*

6 EGG YOLKS

75G (⅓ CUP) CASTER SUGAR

100ML PASSIONFRUIT JUICE (SEE NOTE)

50G BUTTER, CUBED

1   Whisk the egg yolks and sugar in a small saucepan until pale.

2   Place the saucepan over a low heat and add the passionfruit juice and butter.

3   Whisk the mixture until it is frothy, and then stir with a wooden spoon constantly for 5 minutes, or until it coats the back of a spoon. When you swipe your finger across the spoon, the liquid should hold and not drip down through the swipe.

4   Transfer the mixture to a small bowl and refrigerate for at least 1 hour, until cooled and set.

NOTE

To make 100ml passionfruit juice, scoop the pulp of 10–12 passionfruit into a food processor. Process briefly, then strain through a sieve to remove the seeds. I like to return 1 teaspoon of seeds back to the juice, so that it's recognisable as passionfruit juice. If you don't have quite enough juice from the passionfruit, top up with orange juice. By substituting lemon, lime or orange juice for the passionfruit juice, you can make different flavoured curds in the same way.

Dessert Wine Zabaglione

Zabaglione (also known as sabayon) is a creamy dessert made from egg yolks, wine and sugar. It can be flavoured with lemon or vanilla as well. Serve in glasses as the main feature, or over a dessert as an accompaniment. It takes a bit of whisking action but the result is a light, foamy dessert that tastes much more decadent than it is! Do make it just prior to serving.

PREP TIME: *5 minutes*
COOKING TIME: *15 minutes*
MAKES: *4 serves*

6 EGG YOLKS

160ML (⅔ CUP) DESSERT WINE

75G (⅓ CUP) CASTER SUGAR

1 VANILLA BEAN, SPLIT,
SEEDS SCRAPED

250ML (1 CUP)
THICKENED CREAM

AMARETTI BISCUITS, TO SERVE
(SEE NOTE)

1 Fill one-third of a large saucepan with water and bring it to a simmer.

2 Place the egg yolks, dessert wine, sugar and vanilla seeds into a heatproof bowl that will fit snugly over the saucepan. Beat with hand-held beaters until thick and pale, then place the bowl over gently simmering water, ensuring the water does not touch the bottom of the bowl.

3 Beat constantly for about 8–10 minutes, until the mixture has tripled in volume.

4 Remove from the heat and beat a further 2–3 minutes until the mixture has cooled down. Place in the fridge to cool further while you whip the cream.

5 In a separate bowl, whip the cream to firm peaks. Fold it into the zabaglione mixture until just combined.

6 Spoon into 4 elegant glasses and serve Amaretti biscuits on the side, for dipping.

NOTE

Amaretti biscuits are an Italian almond biscuit, available from supermarkets and some green grocers. If you are making your own you could make them in a finger shape so that they are easier for dipping! (see page 235) By omitting the cream you have a dairy-free dessert that tastes like it isn't!

Baked Vanilla Bean Custards

Baked custards are simply custards that are cooked in the oven until they set. I like to bake them in a water bath to give them a silkier texture.

PREP TIME: *15 minutes*
COOKING TIME: *55 minutes*
MAKES: *4 serves*

400ML MILK

300ML POURING CREAM

1 VANILLA BEAN, SPLIT, SEEDS SCRAPED

2 EGGS

5 EGG YOLKS

110G (½ CUP) CASTER SUGAR

1 Preheat oven to 130°C. Grease four 250ml (1 cup) capacity oven-proof ramekins and place them into a large baking dish.

2 Combine the milk, cream, vanilla bean and seeds in a medium saucepan and place over medium heat. Heat until the mixture is steaming. Remove from the heat.

3 Beat the eggs, egg yolks and sugar together in a bowl of an electric mixer on medium speed for 3–4 minutes, until thickened and pale.

4 Reduce the mixer to low speed. Remove the vanilla pod from the cream mixture and discard. Add the vanilla cream mixture to the egg mixture and mix until combined. Strain through a sieve into a jug. Allow the mixture to stand for 3 minutes. A layer of foam will rise to the top. Carefully skim this off and discard (it seems like a waste but most of it is just air, and leaving it on will cause your custards to look sunken).

5 Pour the custard mixture into the ramekins. Pour enough boiling water into the baking dish to come halfway up the sides of the ramekins. Cover the baking dish with aluminium foil.

6 Bake for about 55 minutes, until the surface is set and there is a slight wobble underneath. Carefully remove from the baking dish and stand for 10–15 minutes before serving. Alternatively, cool completely then refrigerate for serving cold later.

NOTE

These are best served warm out of the oven, but they can also be chilled in the refrigerator and eaten cold. They will keep, covered, in the fridge for up to 3 days. Other flavours that would work well in place of the vanilla include cinnamon, nutmeg, ginger or toasted coconut.

Beyond the basics...

Frangelico Zabaglione with White Chocolate Hazelnuts and Fresh Figs

Zabaglione is a great accompaniment for fruit, adding a beautifully creamy element with so much more flavour than cream alone. I think in particular it is a great accompaniment to fresh figs. Sadly, the fig season is short, so when they're out of season poached pears would make a great substitution.

PREP TIME: *10 minutes*
COOKING TIME: *10–13 minutes + setting*
MAKES: *6 serves*

60G HAZELNUTS

150G WHITE CHOCOLATE, CHOPPED

6 EGG YOLKS

100ML FRANGELICO

80G (⅓ CUP) CASTER SUGAR

1 TSP VANILLA EXTRACT

250ML (1 CUP) THICKENED CREAM

6 FRESH FIGS, SLICED

1 Toast the hazelnuts in a dry frying pan over low heat, stirring regularly, until they are lightly coloured and fragrant. Tip them into a clean tea towel and rub as much of their skins off as possible.

2 To make the white chocolate hazelnuts, melt the white chocolate by placing it in a microwave-safe bowl and cooking on high for 30 seconds. Stir and continue cooking in 30-second bursts, stirring in between, until it is melted and smooth. Tip the toasted hazelnuts into the white chocolate and then spoon them out individually onto a flat tray lined with baking paper. Refrigerate for about 15 minutes, until set. Dip each hazelnut into the chocolate a second time and refrigerate again until set. Roughly chop and set aside until needed.

3 For the zabaglione, fill one-third of a large saucepan with water and bring it to a simmer. Place the egg yolks, Frangelico and sugar into a heatproof bowl that will fit snugly over the saucepan. Beat with hand-held beaters until thick and pale, then place the bowl over the gently simmering water, ensuring the water does not touch the bottom of the bowl. Beat constantly for about 8–10 minutes, until the mixture has doubled in volume and will hold a thick ribbon on the surface for a few seconds when the beaters are lifted.

4 Remove from the heat and beat a further 2–3 minutes until the mixture has cooled down a little. Place in the fridge to cool further while you whip the cream.

5 In a separate bowl, whip the cream to firm peaks. Fold it into the zabaglione mixture until just combined.

6 Divide the figs among the serving glasses. Spoon over the zabaglione, and sprinkle with the white chocolate hazelnuts.

NOTE

The zabaglione is best made just prior to serving but can be stored in the fridge for a few hours. (The consistency will be slightly more dense.) The white chocolate hazelnuts can be made ahead of time and stored in an airtight container. By omitting the cream you have a dairy-free dessert that tastes like it isn't!

Blood Orange Baked Custard

I love the tart quality of blood orange, and when combined with a rich, sweet cream, the balance of this dessert seems just right. I've kept the sizes small as it is quite decadent.

PREP TIME: *15 minutes*
COOKING TIME: *45 minutes*
 + 2 hours chilling
MAKES: *6 serves*

2 EGGS

5 EGG YOLKS

110G (½ CUP) CASTER SUGAR

FINELY GRATED ZEST OF
1 BLOOD ORANGE

500ML (2 CUPS) POURING CREAM

180ML (¾ CUP)
BLOOD ORANGE JUICE

3 BLOOD ORANGES, PEELED
AND SEGMENTED, TO SERVE

1 TBS BLANCHED,
SLIVERED PISTACHIOS,
TO SERVE (SEE NOTE)

1 Preheat the oven to 130°C. Grease six 150ml-capacity ovenproof ramekins and place them into a large baking dish.

2 Combine the eggs, egg yolks, sugar and zest in the bowl of an electric mixer and beat on medium speed for 3–4 minutes, until pale and creamy.

3 Reduce the speed to low and add the cream and blood orange juice. Mix until well combined and then pour through a sieve into a jug. Allow the mixture to stand for 5 minutes, then skim the froth from the top and discard (it seems like a waste but most of it is just air and leaving it on will cause your custards to look sunken).

4 Divide the custard mixture evenly among the ramekins. Pour enough boiling water into the baking dish to come halfway up the sides of the ramekins. Cover the baking dish with aluminium foil.

5 Bake for about 45 minutes, until the surface is set and there is a slight wobble underneath. Carefully remove from the baking dish, cool to room temperature then refrigerate for about 2 hours, until set.

6 Serve with blood orange segments on top and sprinkle with the pistachios.

NOTE

These can be made ahead of time and kept in the fridge for up to 3 days. Blanched, slivered pistachios are available from specialty or Middle Eastern food shops. To create different flavoured custards, omit the zest and swap the blood orange juice for espresso coffee, passionfruit juice or coconut milk.

Blueberry Croissant Pudding

I've never been a massive fan of bread and butter pudding, but when it's made with croissants ...well, that's a whole different story!

PREP TIME: *15 minutes + 30 minutes standing*
COOKING TIME: *45-50 minutes*
MAKES: *4 serves*

1 TBS CASTER SUGAR, FOR DUSTING

4 EGGS

180ML (¾ CUP) MILK

180ML (¾ CUP) POURING CREAM

75G (⅓ CUP) CASTER SUGAR

FINELY GRATED ZEST OF 1 ORANGE

4 LARGE CROISSANTS, ABOUT 100G EACH (SEE NOTE)

75G (½ CUP) BLUEBERRIES

1 TBS WHITE SUGAR

GOOD-QUALITY VANILLA ICE CREAM, TO SERVE (SEE PAGE 88)

1   Grease a large ovenproof dish (1 litre capacity) and dust with 1 tablespoon caster sugar, discarding any excess.

2   To make the custard mixture, combine the eggs, milk, cream, sugar and zest in a blender and blend until smooth.

3   Tear the croissants into quarters and place in a single layer in the ovenproof dish, squeezing them in to fit tightly. Sprinkle with the blueberries and pour the custard mixture over them.

4   Let them stand for about 30 minutes, until the croissants have absorbed most of the egg mixture. Meanwhile, preheat the oven to 170°C.

5   Sprinkle the pudding with 1 tablespoon of white sugar. Bake for 45–50 minutes, until it is golden on the top and the custard is set. Serve warm with ice cream.

NOTE

This is best made just before serving, and served warm from the oven. It will keep in the fridge, covered, for up to 3 days but will need to be gently reheated before serving. Supermarkets sell packaged varieties of croissants, which work well in this recipe too, but you will need 8 croissants to make this recipe as they are generally smaller than bakery versions. Just check the total weight.

Spiced Crème Brûlée

This spiced Crème Brûlée reminds me a little of eggnog. Crème Brûlée is simply a custard made with cream that has a caramelised sugar topping. The fun part is cracking through the glassy top to the luscious and creamy treasure underneath. I've kept these a smaller size as they are fairly rich.

PREP TIME: *25 minutes*
COOKING TIME: *40–45 minutes*
 + 2 hours chilling
MAKES: *6 serves*

700ML POURING CREAM

1 TSP GROUND CINNAMON

½ TSP GROUND NUTMEG

¼ TSP GROUND GINGER

¼ TSP GROUND CARDAMOM

1 VANILLA BEAN, SPLIT,
SEEDS SCRAPED

2 EGGS

5 EGG YOLKS

110G (½ CUP) CASTER SUGAR

6–9 TSP CASTER SUGAR, EXTRA

1 Preheat the oven to 130°C. Grease six 150ml-capacity ovenproof ramekins and place them into a large baking dish.

2 Combine the cream, ground spices and the vanilla seeds into a medium saucepan over medium-high heat. Heat, stirring occasionally, until steaming.

3 Beat the eggs, egg yolks and sugar together in a bowl of an electric mixer on medium speed for 3–4 minutes, until thickened and pale.

4 Reduce the speed to low and add the spiced cream. Mix until well combined. Pour into a jug through a sieve. Allow the mixture to stand for 3 minutes. A layer of foam will rise to the top. Carefully skim this off and discard (it seems like a waste but most of it is just air and leaving it on will cause your custards to look sunken. If you don't want to waste the foam, put it in a mug and drink it like eggnog).

5 Divide the custard mixture evenly among the ramekins. Pour enough boiling water into the baking dish to come halfway up the sides of the ramekins. Cover the baking dish with aluminium foil.

6 Bake for 40–45 minutes, until set on the surface with a slight wobble underneath. Remove from the baking dish and set aside to cool to room temperature. Cover with plastic wrap and refrigerate for 2 hours.

7 Just before serving, sprinkle each crème brûlée with ½ teaspoon caster sugar, keeping it an even thickness across the whole surface. Use a kitchen blowtorch to caramelise the sugar, taking care not to hover too long over one spot. Repeat with another ½ teaspoon caster sugar and, if you like, a third layer. The idea is to gradually layer up the caramelised sugar. Leave it to set for 1–2 minutes before serving.

NOTE

These can be made up to the end of step 6 and kept in the fridge for up to 3 days. Kitchen blowtorches are available from kitchenware shops. If you don't have one, you can sprinkle with sugar and place under a hot grill for 1–2 minutes, but the effect is not quite the same!

Lime Curd and Coconut Slice

Lime makes such a beautiful curd, and paired up with coconut in this dessert slice, it's refreshing yet indulgent at the same time. While this is technically a slice, it is one you'll need a fork and plate for, so I like to eat it as a dessert with a large scoop of vanilla ice cream.

PREP TIME: *40 minutes*
COOKING TIME: *35–40 minutes*
REFRIGERATING TIME: *3 hours minimum (preferably overnight)*
MAKES: *12 small (or 6 large) squares*

BASE

150G (1 CUP) PLAIN FLOUR

40G (½ CUP) FLAKED COCONUT

110G (½ CUP) CASTER SUGAR

125G BUTTER, AT ROOM TEMPERATURE, CHOPPED

1 TBS MILK

TOPPING

1 ½ TBS CORNFLOUR

160ML (⅔ CUP) POURING CREAM

6 EGGS

385G (1¾ CUPS) CASTER SUGAR

FINELY GRATED ZEST OF 2 LIMES

180ML (¾ CUP) LIME JUICE (ABOUT 5–6 LIMES)

1 Preheat the oven to 170°C. Grease a 30cm x 20cm (base measurement) slice tin and line the base and sides with baking paper.

2 For the base, place the flour, coconut, sugar, butter and milk into a food processor. Using the pulse button, process in short bursts until the mixture looks like coarse breadcrumbs but will hold together when squeezed between your fingers. Tip the mixture into the tin and spread evenly over the base, pressing down firmly using the heel of your hand (you'll need to use your fingers near the edges). Bake for 25 minutes, until golden brown.

3 For the topping, combine the cornflour and 2 tablespoons of the cream in a small bowl and whisk with a fork until smooth. Put the eggs into a bowl and whisk until they have blended well. Add the remainder of the cream, sugar, zest and juice, and whisk until thoroughly combined. Stir in the cream and cornflour mixture and then tip it all into a medium saucepan. Stir with a whisk over medium heat for 5–6 minutes, until the mixture thickens slightly.

4 Pour the topping over the cooked base and return it to the oven for a further 10–15 minutes, until the surface has set and there is a slight wobble underneath. Cool to room temperature, then refrigerate for at least 3 hours, preferably overnight. Cut into 12 small (or 6 large) pieces to serve.

NOTE

This recipe is best made the day before serving. It keeps in an airtight container in the fridge for up to 1 week. For something different, you could substitute the lime juice for other flavours. Try passionfruit juice or blood orange.

Warm Chocolate Pots

This is a decadent dessert –
perfect for the chocoholic!

PREP TIME: *15 minutes*
COOKING TIME: *40–45 minutes*
MAKES: *6 serves*

375ML (1½ CUPS) MILK

250ML (1 CUP)
THICKENED CREAM

2 TBS DARK COCOA POWDER
(SEE NOTE)

200G GOOD-QUALITY DARK
CHOCOLATE, FINELY CHOPPED

6 EGG YOLKS

1 TBS CASTER SUGAR

1   Preheat the oven to 130°C, and lightly grease six 150ml ovenproof ramekins. Place them into a large baking dish.

2   Combine the milk and cream in a medium saucepan and place over medium heat. Heat until the mixture is steaming and then take it off the heat. Add the cocoa powder and dark chocolate and stir until the chocolate is melted and the mixture is smooth.

3   Place the egg yolks and sugar into the bowl of an electric mixer and beat until smooth. With the beaters on slow speed, add a little of the chocolate mixture and mix until well combined. Add the remainder of the chocolate mixture and mix until well combined.

4   Pour the mixture through a sieve into a jug. Divide the mixture evenly among the ramekins. Pour enough boiling water into the baking dish to come halfway up the side of the ramekins. Cover the baking dish with aluminium foil.

5   Bake for 40–45 minutes, until the surface is set and there is a slight wobble beneath it. Remove the ramekins from the baking dish and stand for 10 minutes before serving.

NOTE

Dark cocoa powder is also known as Dutch or Dutch-processed cocoa. It has a rich, deep colour and flavour, and is available from delis and specialty food shops. These pots can be refrigerated for up to a week and served cold at a later time, like a chocolate crème brûlée. If you would like White Chocolate Pots, simply omit the cocoa powder and swap the dark chocolate for the same amount of white chocolate.

The basics...

Simple Vanilla Ice Cream

Homemade 'Ice Magic'

Special Occasion
Vanilla Bean Ice Cream

Chocolate Sorbet

Zesty Lemon Sorbet

Beyond the basics...

Berry Compote with Baileys
Ice Cream and Dark Chocolate
and Hazelnut Crumb

Baileys Ice Cream

Toasted Coconut Ice Cream

Caramelised Banana with
Toasted Coconut Ice Cream and
White Chocolate Peanuts

Frozen Tiramisu

Mascarpone Ice Cream

Peanut Butter Ice Cream

Peanut Butter and Chocolate
Ice Cream Sandwich

Vanilla Roasted Cherries with
Rich Milk Chocolate Ice Cream
and Toasted Almonds

Rich Milk Chocolate Ice Cream

Passionfruit Ice Cream

Passionfruit Splice with
Pineapple Carpaccio

Toffee Apple Sorbet

Ice creams & sorbets

Dripping down the side of a cone, melting over another dessert or snuck from the freezer when you're home alone, ice cream and sorbets are indispensable in the dessert world.

They are the perfect vehicle for creativity. When you make your own, you are 100% in the driver's seat, making decisions on flavour and texture. Once you've mastered a base recipe, you're free to infuse, add or stir through just about any ingredient that takes your fancy.

Each of the recipes in this chapter requires the use of an ice cream churn. In order to achieve a smooth, luxurious texture, the base mixtures need to be frozen quickly and kept on the move so that the ice crystals formed inside them are kept small. An ice cream churn is built for this job!

There are a few extra tips that will assist you in getting the best results:

- Allow yourself plenty of time – the best results come when you have time to chill everything properly.

- Know that the amount of sugar, alcohol and salt in a mixture all have an effect on the way a mixture freezes. So don't play around with those figures too much!

- Because homemade ice creams and sorbets are made from fresh ingredients without the use of chemicals or preservatives, they melt more quickly than many store-bought varieties. You need to know this so you can plan to eat them quickly as soon as they come out of the freezer.

Simple Vanilla Ice Cream

This is the simplest way I know to make a tasty ice cream. The beauty of this recipe is that you can use it as a base recipe for a multitude of other flavourings. A favourite with my kids (and me) is to keep it plain and serve it with some homemade 'Ice Magic' (page 90).

PREP TIME: *10 minutes + chilling*
COOKING TIME: *10 minutes*
FREEZING TIME: *2 hours minimum (preferably overnight)*
MAKES: *6–8 serves*

250ML (1 CUP) MILK

250ML (1 CUP) POURING CREAM

1 TSP VANILLA EXTRACT

6 EGG YOLKS

110G (1 CUP) CASTER SUGAR

HOMEMADE 'ICE MAGIC' TO SERVE (SEE PAGE 90)

1   Combine the milk, cream and vanilla extract in a medium saucepan and heat over medium heat until it is steaming. Meanwhile, whisk the egg yolks and sugar in a bowl until thick and pale.

2   Gradually pour the hot milk mixture into the egg mixture, whisking continuously. Rinse out the saucepan to remove any milk sediment and then tip the mixture back into the saucepan through a sieve.

3   Cook over medium heat, stirring constantly, until the mixture is thick enough to coat the back of a spoon (when you swipe your finger across the spoon, the liquid holds and does not drip down through the swipe). This can take 5–10 minutes, depending on your stove. Take care not to boil or the mixture will curdle.

4   Transfer to a bowl and cool the mixture to room temperature, then chill until very cold. You can speed up this process by transferring the mixture to a stainless steel bowl placed over another bowl of ice and a splash of water, and then refrigerating for 2–3 hours, stirring occasionally.

5   Churn the mixture in an ice cream churn, according to the manufacturer's instructions. Transfer to an airtight container, and freeze for at least 2 hours, but preferably overnight. Serve with homemade 'Ice Magic'.

NOTE

This recipe is best made the day before serving. It will keep for up to 1 week in the freezer.

Homemade 'Ice Magic'

The child in me still loves the magic of an ice cream topping that hardens before my eyes. And I still love cracking it with my spoon before savouring the timeless combination of rich chocolate and vanilla ice cream.

PREP TIME: *3 minutes*
COOKING TIME: *2 minutes*
MAKES: *150ml*

50G MILK CHOCOLATE, CHOPPED

50G DARK CHOCOLATE, CHOPPED

50G COPHA, CHOPPED

1   Combine the milk chocolate, dark chocolate and Copha in a microwave-safe bowl. Cook on high in 30-second bursts, stirring between each burst, until all the chocolate and Copha is melted. Stir well.

2   Pour onto ice cream and watch it set before your eyes!

NOTE

This can be made ahead of time and stored in the fridge, but it will need to be warmed gently to get it back to pouring consistency.

Special Occasion Vanilla Bean Ice Cream

Admittedly, this ice cream takes a bit more time and effort, but what you get at the end is a richer, smoother, glossier ice cream. It's not one I'd make for everyday eating, but when you want your ice cream to be the best it can be this is the recipe I'd go for.

PREP TIME: *30 minutes + chilling*
COOKING TIME: *15 minutes*
FREEZING TIME: *2 hours minimum (preferably overnight)*
MAKES: *6 serves (see photograph on page 93)*

250ML (1 CUP) MILK

250ML (1 CUP) POURING CREAM

1 VANILLA BEAN, SPLIT, SEEDS SCRAPED

6 EGG YOLKS

110G (½ CUP) CASTER SUGAR

1 Combine the milk, cream and vanilla bean and seeds in a medium saucepan and heat over medium heat until it is steaming.

2 Use electric beaters to whisk the egg yolks and sugar in a large heatproof bowl for 2–3 minutes, until thick and pale.

3 Remove the vanilla bean from the milk mixture and gradually pour the hot milk mixture into the egg mixture, whisking at low speed continuously.

4 Place this bowl of mixture over a saucepan of gently simmering water (ensuring that the bottom of the bowl is not touching the water). Whisk for 3 minutes on low speed, then a further 7–12 minutes on medium speed until the mixture has thickened and reached 85°C. If you don't have a thermometer, the mixture should be too hot to leave your finger in there!

5 Transfer to a cold bowl and cool the mixture to room temperature, then chill until very cold over another bowl of ice and a splash of water.

6 Churn the mixture in an ice cream churn, according to the manufacturer's instructions. Transfer to an airtight container and freeze for at least 2 hours, but preferably overnight.

NOTE

This recipe is best made the day before serving. It will keep for up to 1 week in the freezer.

Chocolate Sorbet

In my opinion, if you're going to eat chocolate, it might as well be a good hit of chocolate! This sorbet is rich and delivers a hit as good as any intense chocolate dessert.

PREP TIME: *5 minutes + chilling*
COOKING TIME: *5 minutes*
FREEZING TIME: *4 hours minimum (preferably overnight)*
MAKES: *750ml*

500ML (2 CUPS) WATER

220G (1 CUP) CASTER SUGAR

50G (½ CUP) DARK COCOA POWDER (SEE NOTE)

100G GOOD-QUALITY DARK CHOCOLATE, GRATED

¼ TSP VANILLA EXTRACT

1 Combine the water and sugar in a medium saucepan and stir over low heat, without boiling, until the sugar has dissolved. Add the cocoa powder and whisk until smooth.

2 Take the saucepan off the heat and add the grated chocolate and vanilla extract. Stir continuously until the chocolate has melted.

3 Cool the mixture to room temperature. You can speed up this process by transferring the mixture to a stainless steel bowl placed over another bowl of ice and a splash of water, and stand for 20–30 minutes, stirring occasionally. Refrigerate overnight, until well chilled.

4 Churn the mixture in an ice cream churn, according to the manufacturer's instructions. Transfer to an airtight container and freeze for at least 4 hours, but preferably overnight.

NOTE

You need to start this recipe 1–2 days before serving. Sorbets are best eaten within 1–2 days of freezing, otherwise they begin to go icy. Homemade sorbets melt very quickly once out of the freezer. If you need this to be completely dairy-free, simply substitute an extra tablespoon of dark cocoa powder for the dark chocolate. Dark cocoa powder is also known as Dutch or Dutch-processed cocoa. It has a rich, deep colour and flavour, and is available from delis and specialty food shops.

Zesty Lemon Sorbet

I love a good hit of lemon, and what better way to experience it than this? It's especially cooling on a hot summer's day, but I'll take this palate cleanser any time of year.

PREP TIME: *10 minutes + chilling*
COOKING TIME: *5 minutes*
FREEZING TIME: *4 hours minimum (preferably overnight)*
MAKES: *1 litre*

500G CASTER SUGAR

500ML (2 CUPS) WATER

80ML (⅓ CUP) GLUCOSE SYRUP

2 TSP VERY FINELY GRATED LEMON ZEST

800ML FRESH LEMON JUICE (ABOUT 10 MEDIUM LEMONS)

1   Combine the sugar, water and glucose syrup in a medium saucepan and stir over medium-low heat, without boiling, until the sugar has dissolved. Increase the heat, and simmer for 1 minute. Add the zest, and then take the pan off the heat and stand for 10 minutes.

2   Stir the lemon juice into the sugar syrup. Cool the mixture to room temperature. You can speed up this process by transferring the mixture to a stainless steel bowl placed over another bowl of ice and a splash of water. Stand for 20–30 minutes, stirring occasionally.

3   Strain the mixture to remove the zest, then refrigerate overnight or until well chilled.

4   Churn the mixture in an ice cream churn, according to the manufacturer's instructions. Transfer to an airtight container and freeze for at least 4 hours, but preferably overnight.

NOTE

You need to start this recipe 1–2 days before serving. Sorbets are best eaten within 1–2 days of freezing, otherwise they begin to go icy. Homemade sorbets melt very quickly once out of the freezer – so eat quickly! This recipe could be used as a basic recipe for other zesty flavours. For something a bit different try mandarin, blood orange or lime.

Beyond the basics…

Berry Compote with Baileys Ice Cream and Dark Chocolate and Hazelnut Crumb

PREP TIME: *15 minutes*

COOKING TIME: *10 minutes*

MAKES: *6 serves*

125ML (½ CUP) FRESH ORANGE JUICE

125ML (½ CUP) WATER

2 TBS CASTER SUGAR

1 TSP LEMON JUICE

300G (2 CUPS) FROZEN MIXED BERRIES

60G HAZELNUTS

80G DARK CHOCOLATE, ROUGHLY CHOPPED

1 QUANTITY OF BAILEYS ICE CREAM (SEE FOLLOWING PAGE)

1 To make the berry compote, combine the orange juice, water and sugar in a small saucepan. Stir over medium heat until the sugar has dissolved. Increase the heat to bring to a simmer. Cook, without stirring, for 5–7 minutes, until the liquid thickens slightly. Remove from the heat and stand for 5 minutes to cool slightly. Stir in the lemon juice.

2 Place the berries into a heatproof bowl. Pour the liquid over the berries and leave to come to room temperature.

3 Meanwhile, toast the hazelnuts in a dry frying pan until they are fragrant and lightly browned. Tip into a clean tea towel and rub as much of their skins off as possible. Cool to room temperature.

4 Combine the cooled hazelnuts and the dark chocolate in the bowl of a food processor. Blitz in short bursts until they are coarse crumbs. Be careful not to blitz in long bursts or for too long as the chocolate might melt!

5 To serve, divide the berries among 6 serving bowls or glasses. Top with a generous scoop of Baileys ice cream and sprinkle with the chocolate hazelnut crumb.

NOTE

Each of these components can be made ahead of time and kept in airtight containers. Keep the compote in the fridge and bring it back to room temperature before serving.

Baileys Ice Cream

Because Baileys is one of life's little indulgences, it's worth the effort to use the ice cream technique that will give you the richest, smoothest result. It may be a little bit more work, but when you sit down with it in front of you, you'll be pleased you went the extra mile.

PREP TIME: *30 minutes + chilling*
COOKING TIME: *15 minutes*
FREEZING TIME: *2 hours minimum (preferably overnight)*
MAKES: *6 serves*

250ML (1 CUP) MILK

250ML (1 CUP) POURING CREAM

60ML (¼ CUP)
BAILEYS IRISH CREAM

6 EGG YOLKS

110G (½ CUP) CASTER SUGAR

1 TBS BAILEYS, EXTRA

1   Place the milk, cream and Baileys into a medium saucepan and heat over medium heat until steaming.

2   Use electric beaters to whisk the egg yolks and sugar in a large heatproof bowl for 2–3 minutes, until thick and pale. Gradually pour the hot milk mixture into the egg mixture, whisking constantly at low speed.

3   Place this bowl of mixture over a saucepan of gently simmering water (ensuring that the bottom of the bowl is not touching the water). Whisk for 3 minutes on low speed, then a further 7–12 minutes on medium speed, until the mixture has thickened and reached 85°C. If you don't have a thermometer, the mixture should be too hot to leave your finger in there!

4   Transfer to a cold bowl and cool the mixture to room temperature, then chill until very cold over another bowl of ice and a splash of water.

5   Stir in the extra Baileys. Churn the mixture in an ice cream churn, according to the manufacturer's instructions. Transfer to an airtight container and freeze for at least 2 hours, but preferably overnight.

NOTE

This recipe is best made the day before serving. It will keep for up to 1 week in the freezer. Other liqueurs would work just as well for this dish. Try Cointreau, Kahlua or Frangelico.

Toasted Coconut Ice Cream

One way to create flavour in an
ice cream is to infuse the milk
and cream base with a flavour
before you add the eggs. This
one is infused with toasted
coconut. It would be a delicious
creamy accompaniment to
the Tropical Fruit Salad with
Lemongrass Syrup (page 26), or
you could serve it as I have with
Caramelised Banana and White
Chocolate Peanuts (page 102).

PREP TIME: *30 minutes + chilling*
COOKING TIME: *10 minutes*
FREEZING TIME: *2 hours minimum
 (preferably overnight)*
MAKES: *6 serves*

45G (½ CUP) COCONUT FLAKES

250ML (1 CUP) MILK

250ML (1 CUP) POURING CREAM

1 TSP COCONUT ESSENCE

5 EGG YOLKS

110G (½ CUP) CASTER SUGAR

1 Place the coconut flakes in a non-stick frying pan and dry-fry them over a medium heat, shaking the pan regularly, until they are a deep golden colour.

2 Meanwhile, combine the milk, cream and coconut essence in a medium saucepan. Place over a medium heat and heat until it is steaming.

3 Tip the toasted coconut into the hot milk and turn off the heat. Stand for 15 minutes to allow the flavours to infuse. Strain off the coconut and discard. Return the milk to a medium heat until steaming again.

4 Whisk the egg yolks and sugar in a bowl until thick and pale. Gradually pour the hot milk mixture into the egg mixture, whisking continuously.

5 Rinse out the saucepan to remove any milk sediment and then tip the mixture back into the saucepan through a sieve.

6 Cook over a medium heat, stirring constantly, until the mixture is thick enough to coat the back of a spoon (when you swipe your finger across the spoon, the liquid holds and does not drip down through the swipe). This can take 5–10 minutes, depending on your stove. Take care not to boil, or the mixture will curdle.

7 Transfer to a bowl and cool the mixture to room temperature, then chill until very cold. You can speed up this process by transferring the mixture to a stainless steel bowl placed over another bowl of ice and a splash of water, and then refrigerating for 2–3 hours, stirring occasionally.

8 Churn the mixture in an ice cream churn, according to the manufacturer's instructions. Transfer to an airtight container, and freeze for at least 2 hours, but preferably overnight.

NOTE

*This recipe is best made the day before serving. It will keep for up to
1 week in the freezer. You can use the same process for other flavours.
Try infusing the milk with cinnamon, mint, Earl Grey tea, ginger or
toasted sesame seeds.*

Caramelised Banana with Toasted Coconut Ice Cream and White Chocolate Peanuts (Luke's favourite)

PREP TIME: *10 minutes*
COOKING TIME: *8 minutes*
MAKES: *6 serves*

70G (½ CUP) UNSALTED
ROASTED PEANUTS

50G WHITE CHOCOLATE,
CHOPPED

3 MEDIUM BANANAS,
NOT TOO RIPE

2½ TBS CASTER SUGAR

20G BUTTER

TOASTED COCONUT ICE CREAM
(SEE PREVIOUS PAGE), TO SERVE

1 Line a baking tray with non-stick baking paper.

2 Toast the peanuts in a small frying pan over medium heat for 4–5 minutes, until fragrant and lightly golden. Shake the pan regularly to ensure even colouring.

3 To make the white chocolate peanuts, place the white chocolate into a microwave-safe bowl. Microwave on high in short bursts of 30 seconds, stirring between each, until melted. Add the peanuts to the chocolate and stir to coat them well. Tip onto the prepared tray and leave to set (you can speed up this process by putting it into the fridge). Chop roughly into chunky pieces.

4 For the caramelised banana, peel the bananas and slice diagonally into 5–8mm thick slices. Sprinkle each slice liberally with caster sugar and allow them to sit for 5 minutes to absorb some of the sugar. Heat a large frying pan over medium heat. Add the butter and, once melted, place the banana slices into the butter, sugared-side down. Cook for 1–2 minutes until golden brown. Flip them over and cook for a further 10 seconds to heat through. Spoon onto serving plates.

5 Top the caramelised bananas with a large scoop of toasted coconut ice cream, and scatter with white chocolate peanuts.

Frozen Tiramisu

PREP TIME: *15 minutes*
FREEZING TIME: *2 hours minimum (preferably overnight)*
MAKES: *6 serves*

1 QUANTITY OF MASCARPONE ICE CREAM, FRESHLY CHURNED (SEE FOLLOWING PAGE)

250ML (1 CUP) ESPRESSO COFFEE

250ML (1 CUP) KAHLUA

330G SPONGE FINGER (SAVOIARDI) BISCUITS

1 Spray a 25cm x 9cm (base measurement) loaf tin with oil spray and line the base with baking paper, extending over the two long sides. Spoon one quarter of the mascarpone ice cream onto the base of the tin.

2 Combine the coffee and Kahlua in a bowl that is just big enough to dip the biscuits into. Dip 2 sponge finger biscuits at a time into the coffee mixture, holding them under the liquid for 5–10 seconds. Lay them on top of the mascarpone layer to create a sponge layer (the biscuits need to be very close together and some may need trimming to fit).

3 Use a pastry brush to apply another coating of the coffee mixture onto each biscuit, taking care not to get any on the ice cream, as it will thin the consistency. Spoon another quarter of the mascarpone ice cream onto the sponge finger layer.

4 Repeat the sponge finger layer, dipping and brushing again. Spoon another quarter of the mascarpone ice cream onto the second sponge finger layer.

5 Create one last sponge finger layer, dipping and brushing again. Spoon the remaining mascarpone ice cream onto the final sponge finger layer.

6 Cover the loaf tin with plastic wrap and freeze for a minimum of 2 hours, but preferably overnight.

7 Loosen the edges of the frozen tiramisu by running a knife around any places where it appears to be stuck. Invert onto a board and remove the baking paper. Slice each end off to neaten it.

8 To serve, place a thick slice of the frozen tiramisu onto each serving plate.

NOTE

This recipe is best made the day before serving. It will keep for up to a week in the freezer.

Mascarpone Ice Cream

Mascarpone adds a depth of flavour that other creams just don't have. This ice cream is beautiful served with the Pear, Maple and Macadamia Upside-Down Cake (see page 202), or with a rich, dark chocolate tart. You could also do as I've done and indulge your love of retro desserts by turning it into a frozen Tiramisu (see page 104).

PREP TIME: *30 minutes + chilling*
COOKING TIME: *10 minutes*
FREEZING TIME: *2 hours minimum (preferably overnight)*
MAKES: *6 serves*

375ML (1½ CUPS) MILK

125ML (½ CUP) POURING CREAM

1 TSP VANILLA EXTRACT

6 EGG YOLKS

150G (⅔ CUP) CASTER SUGAR

250G (1 CUP) MASCARPONE

1   Combine the milk, cream and vanilla extract in a medium saucepan. Place over a medium heat and heat until it is steaming. Meanwhile, whisk the egg yolks and sugar in a bowl until thick and pale.

2   Gradually pour the hot milk mixture into the egg mixture, whisking continuously. Rinse out the saucepan to remove any milk sediment and then tip the mixture back into the saucepan through a sieve.

3   Cook over medium heat, stirring constantly, until the mixture is thick enough to coat the back of a spoon (when you swipe your finger across the spoon, the liquid holds and does not drip down through the swipe). This can take 5–10 minutes, depending on your stove. Take care not to boil, or the mixture will curdle.

4   Transfer to a bowl and cool the mixture to room temperature, then chill until very cold. You can speed up this process by transferring the mixture to a stainless steel bowl placed over another bowl of ice and a splash of water, and then refrigerating for 2–3 hours, stirring occasionally.

5   Place the mascarpone into the bowl of an electric mixer and beat on low until smooth and creamy. With the beaters still on low, gradually add the egg mixture and stir until well combined. Chill again until very cold.

6   Churn in an ice cream machine, according to the manufacturer's instructions. Transfer to an airtight container and freeze for at least 2 hours, but preferably overnight.

NOTE

This recipe is best made the day before serving. It will keep for up to 1 week in the freezer. For different flavours, try swapping the mascarpone with cream cheese or crème fraîche.

Peanut Butter Ice Cream

PREP TIME: *10 minutes + chilling*
COOKING TIME: *10 minutes*
FREEZING TIME: *2½ hours minimum*
 (preferably overnight)
MAKES: *6–8 serves*

250ML (1 CUP) MILK

250ML (1 CUP) POURING CREAM

1 TSP VANILLA EXTRACT

6 EGG YOLKS

110G (½ CUP) CASTER SUGAR

125G (½ CUP)
SMOOTH PEANUT BUTTER

1 Combine the milk, cream and vanilla in a medium saucepan. Place over medium heat and heat until it is steaming. Meanwhile, whisk the egg yolks and sugar in a bowl until thick and pale.

2 Gradually pour the hot milk mixture into the egg mixture, whisking continuously. Rinse out the saucepan to remove any milk sediment and then tip the mixture back into the saucepan through a sieve.

3 Cook over a medium heat, stirring constantly, until the mixture is thick enough to coat the back of a spoon (when you swipe your finger across the spoon, the liquid holds and does not drip down through the swipe). This can take 5–10 minutes, depending on your stove. Take care not to boil, or the mixture will curdle. Add the peanut butter and stir until smooth.

4 Transfer to a bowl and cool the mixture to room temperature, then chill until very cold. You can speed up this process by transferring the mixture to a stainless steel bowl placed over another bowl of ice and a splash of water, and then refrigerating for 2–3 hours, stirring occasionally.

5 Churn the mixture in an ice cream churn, according to the manufacturer's instructions. Transfer to an airtight container and freeze for at least 2½ hours, but preferably overnight.

NOTE

This recipe is best made the day before serving. It will keep for up to 1 week in the freezer. For a different flavour, this recipe would also work if you substituted the peanut butter for chocolate hazelnut spread.

Peanut Butter and Chocolate Ice Cream Sandwich

Anyone who has visited the United States knows that peanut butter and chocolate is a common combination in their confectionery. And I know why – it's simple, but it tastes great!

PREP TIME: *20 minutes*
COOKING TIME: *15 minutes*
FREEZING TIME: *2 hours minimum*
MAKES: *12*

1 QUANTITY OF PEANUT BUTTER
ICE CREAM, FRESHLY CHURNED
(PAGE 107)

300G PKT CAREME DARK
CHOCOLATE SHORTCRUST PASTRY
(SEE NOTE)

1 EGG WHITE, LIGHTLY BEATEN

100G DARK CHOCOLATE

100G MILK CHOCOLATE

1 Line a 26cm x 16cm (base measurement) slice tin with baking paper, extending over the two long sides. Pour the freshly churned ice cream into the tray and freeze for at least 2 hours.

2 To make the biscuits, preheat the oven to 170°C. Line 2 large baking trays with baking paper.

3 Unroll the pastry onto a lightly floured bench and cut into 24 rectangles measuring 6cm x 4cm each. Place the rectangles onto the prepared trays and brush each one with egg white, using a pastry brush. Bake for 15 minutes, then cool on the trays. Store in an airtight container until required.

4 Once the ice cream is frozen, remove it from the tin and place onto a chopping board. Trim the edges and cut out 12 rectangles, measuring 6cm x 4cm.

5 Place each ice cream rectangle onto a cooled pastry rectangle and top with another cooled pastry rectangle. Place in an airtight container and immediately return to the freezer.

6 Break the dark and milk chocolate into small pieces. Place into a microwave-safe bowl and heat on high in a microwave for 30 seconds and then stir. Continue to microwave in 30-second bursts, stirring in between, until it is all melted and smooth. Allow the chocolate to cool slightly for 5 minutes.

7 Working quickly, dip one end of each peanut butter sandwich into the chocolate. Rest at an angle over a chopstick which is placed on baking paper in a large airtight container (to prevent a flat bottom) and return to the freezer as quickly as possible.

8 Store the ice cream sandwiches in the freezer until ready to serve.

NOTE

These can be made ahead of time and kept in the freezer. They are best eaten within 3 days. Careme is a brand of pastry that is handmade and very good-quality. It is available from some supermarkets and specialty food stores. Alternatively, sandwich scoops of the ice cream between your favourite purchased chocolate biscuits.

Vanilla Roasted Cherries with Rich Milk Chocolate Ice Cream and Toasted Almonds

PREP TIME: *10 minutes*

COOKING TIME: *10 minutes*

MAKES: *6 serves*

250G (1¼ CUPS) DRAINED PITTED MORELLO CHERRIES (SEE NOTE)

2 TBS CASTER SUGAR

1 VANILLA BEAN, SPLIT, SEEDS SCRAPED

70G (½ CUP) SLIVERED ALMONDS

RICH MILK CHOCOLATE ICE CREAM, TO SERVE (SEE FOLLOWING PAGE)

1 Preheat the oven to 180°C.

2 Place the cherries into a bowl. Sprinkle with the sugar and add the vanilla bean and seeds. Toss to coat evenly, then pour into a lightly greased ovenproof dish.

3 Bake for 10 minutes, until warmed through and the sugar has dissolved.

4 Meanwhile, place the almonds into a medium frying pan and dry-fry, shaking the pan occasionally, until they are golden and fragrant.

5 To serve, place quenelles (or scoops) of chocolate ice cream into serving bowls. Scatter the baked cherries and toasted almonds over and around the ice cream.

NOTE

Both elements can be made ahead of time but are best if made fresh just before serving. Morello cherries are available in jars at the supermarket.

Rich Milk Chocolate Ice Cream

Chocolate ice cream is a classic flavour, but by using Couverture chocolate as your star ingredient you can take it to a whole new level!

PREP TIME: *30 minutes + chilling*
COOKING TIME: *15 minutes*
FREEZING TIME: *2 hours minimum (preferably overnight)*
MAKES: *6 serves*

250ML (1 CUP) MILK

250ML (1 CUP) POURING CREAM

6 EGG YOLKS

110G (½ CUP) CASTER SUGAR

200G COUVERTURE MILK CHOCOLATE (SEE NOTE), FINELY CHOPPED OR GRATED

1 Place the milk and cream into a medium saucepan and heat over medium heat until it is steaming.

2 Use electric beaters to whisk the egg yolks and sugar in a large heatproof bowl for 2–3 minutes, until thick and pale. Gradually pour the hot milk mixture into the egg mixture, whisking constantly at low speed.

3 Place this bowl of mixture over a saucepan of gently simmering water (ensuring that the bottom of the bowl is not touching the water). Whisk for 3 minutes on low speed, then a further 7–12 minutes on medium speed, until the mixture has thickened and reached 85°C. If you don't have a thermometer, the mixture should be too hot to leave your finger in there!

4 Add the chocolate and stir until it is melted and smooth, then remove the bowl from the heat.

5 Transfer to a cold bowl and cool the mixture to room temperature, then chill until very cold over another bowl of ice and a splash of water.

6 Churn in an ice cream machine, according to the manufacturer's instructions. Transfer to an airtight container and freeze for at least 2 hours, but preferably overnight.

NOTE

This recipe is best made the day before serving. It will keep for up to 1 week in the freezer. Couverture chocolate is very good-quality chocolate, which sets beautifully. It is available from specialty food shops. For something slightly different, use dark or white chocolate in place of the milk chocolate.

Passionfruit Ice Cream

Passionfruit is a wonderfully fresh flavour. It works well with fruit salad but I quite like turning it into a splice to remind me of childhood ice cream treats.

PREP TIME: *30 minutes + chilling*
COOKING TIME: *10 minutes*
FREEZING TIME: *2 hours minimum (preferably overnight)*
MAKES: *6 serves*

10–12 PASSIONFRUIT (DEPENDING ON SIZE)

250ML (1 CUP) MILK

250ML (1 CUP) POURING CREAM

6 EGG YOLKS

110G (½ CUP) CASTER SUGAR

1 Place the pulp from the passionfruit into the bowl of a hand-held stick blender or food processor. Blend with the blade attachment until runny. Pour through a sieve to remove the seeds. Measure the juice – you will need 125ml (½ cup). Stir ½ teaspoon of the seeds back into the juice.

2 Combine the milk and cream in a medium saucepan. Place over a medium heat and heat until it is steaming. Whisk the egg yolks and sugar in a bowl until thick and pale.

3 Gradually pour the hot milk mixture into the egg mixture, whisking continuously. Rinse out the saucepan to remove any milk sediment and then tip the mixture back into the saucepan through a sieve. Add the passionfruit juice.

4 Cook over medium heat, stirring constantly, until the mixture is thick enough to coat the back of a spoon (when you swipe your finger across the spoon, the liquid holds and does not drip down through the swipe). This can take 5–10 minutes, depending on your stove. Take care not to boil, or the mixture will curdle.

5 Transfer to a bowl and cool the mixture to room temperature, then chill until very cold. You can speed up this process by transferring the mixture to a stainless steel bowl placed over another bowl of ice and a splash of water, and then refrigerating for 2–3 hours, stirring occasionally.

6 Churn the mixture in an ice cream churn, according to the manufacturer's instructions. Transfer to an airtight container, and freeze for at least 2 hours before serving, but preferably overnight.

NOTE

This recipe is best made the day before serving. It will keep for up to 1 week in the freezer.

Passionfruit Splice with Pineapple Carpaccio

PREP TIME: *15 minutes + chilling*
COOKING TIME: *10 minutes*
FREEZING TIME: *4–6 hours*
+ overnight
MAKES: *8 serves*

1 QUANTITY OF SIMPLE VANILLA
ICE CREAM (PAGE 88)

1 QUANTITY OF PASSIONFRUIT
ICE CREAM, FRESHLY CHURNED
(SEE PREVIOUS PAGE)

PULP OF 6 PASSIONFRUIT

150G (⅔ CUP) CASTER SUGAR

160ML (⅔ CUP) WATER

½ SWEET PINEAPPLE,
AT ROOM TEMPERATURE

½ TSP SEA SALT FLAKES

1 SPRIG OF MINT, LEAVES
REMOVED AND VERY FINELY
SLICED

1 Remove the vanilla ice cream from the freezer and allow it to sit for 5 minutes to soften.

2 Line an 18cm square cake tin with baking paper, extending over 2 sides.

3 For the base layer, spread the vanilla ice cream into the tin, smoothing out the surface as much as possible to make an even layer. Cover and freeze for 2–3 hours or until firm.

4 For the middle layer, spread the passionfruit ice cream evenly onto the firm vanilla ice cream layer. Cover and freeze for 2–3 hours or until firm.

5 Meanwhile, for the top layer, spoon the passionfruit pulp into the bowl of a hand-held stick blender or food processor. Blend with the blade attachment until runny.

6 Combine the sugar and water in a small saucepan and stir over low heat until the sugar has dissolved. Increase the heat to medium and simmer the mixture for 1 minute.

7 Strain the passionfruit pulp into the sugar syrup. Return ½ teaspoon of seeds back into the syrup and discard the rest. Cool the mixture and refrigerate until cold.

8 Pour the chilled passionfruit mixture onto the firm passionfruit ice cream layer. Cover and freeze overnight.

9 Just prior to serving, peel the pineapple, removing all the eyes. Slice in half lengthways, then cut into very thin slices (about 1mm thick). Lay a few slices of pineapple onto each serving plate. Sprinkle with sea salt and finely shredded mint leaves.

10 Remove the ice cream splice from the freezer and lift out onto a chopping board. Cut into 8 slices and serve with the pineapple.

NOTE

The passionfruit splice needs to be made the day before serving, but will keep in the freezer for up to 3 days. The pineapple carpaccio is best prepared just before serving. You can use 1 litre of good-quality purchased vanilla ice cream, if you like.

Toffee Apple Sorbet

As a child the only fruit I happily ate was apple. So my eyes nearly popped out of my head if Mum ever bought us a toffee apple. What wonderful memories! Here, I've used the flavours to make a grown-up version of this treat.

PREP TIME: *20 minutes + chilling*
COOKING TIME: *15 minutes*
FREEZING TIME: *4 hours minimum (preferably overnight)*
MAKES: *750ml*

4–5 GRANNY SMITH APPLES (OR 250ML/1 CUP APPLE JUICE)

2 TSP LEMON JUICE

330G (1½ CUPS) CASTER SUGAR

125ML (½ CUP) WATER

60ML (¼ CUP) HOT WATER, EXTRA

TOFFEE SHARDS

165G (¾ CUP) CASTER SUGAR

125ML (½ CUP) WATER

1 To prepare the apple juice, juice the apples and stir in the lemon juice immediately. Leave it to sit for 10 minutes for the sediment to rise to the top, then spoon the sediment off the top and measure out 1 cup of juice.

2 For the sugar syrup, combine the sugar and water in a medium saucepan. Stir over a low heat, without boiling, until the sugar has dissolved. Brush down the sides of the saucepan with a pastry brush dipped in water to wash any sugar crystals back into the mixture. Increase the heat to medium and cook, without stirring, for 1 minute. Pour 250ml (1 cup) of the sugar syrup into a heatproof container and set aside. You will have syrup left over, which will become the toffee syrup.

3 For the toffee syrup, brush the sides of the saucepan down again with the pastry brush dipped in water, ensuring the side of the pan is free from sugar crystals. Return the remaining mixture to a medium heat and cook for about 7 minutes, without stirring, until it becomes a rich golden caramel colour. Then take it off the heat and add the hot water. Take care, as it will react violently! Stir until it is combined and smooth (place over the heat again to dissolve lumps, if necessary). If crystals have formed, simply strain them off.

4 Combine the apple juice, sugar syrup and toffee syrup in a bowl, and mix to combine. Refrigerate overnight or until well chilled.

5 Churn the mixture in an ice cream churn, according to the manufacturer's instructions. Transfer to an airtight container and freeze for at least 4 hours, but preferably overnight.

6 For the toffee shards, combine the sugar and water in a medium saucepan. Stir over low heat, without boiling, until the sugar has dissolved. Brush down the sides of the saucepan with a pastry brush dipped in water to wash any sugar crystals back into the mixture. Increase the heat to medium, and cook, without stirring, until it becomes a rich golden caramel colour. Tip the mixture onto a tray lined with baking paper and set aside for about 10 minutes to set. Break into shards.

7 Scoop the ice cream into serving glasses and top with a shard of toffee.

NOTE

You need to start this recipe 1–2 days before serving. Sorbets are best eaten within 1–2 days of freezing, otherwise they begin to go icy. Homemade sorbets melt very quickly once out of the freezer, so eat quickly!

The basics...

Peach & Champagne
Granita

Rose, Raspberry and
Pistachio Frozen Nougat

Choc-Dipped Frozen Fruit on a Stick

Individual Chocolate and
Hazelnut Semi-Freddo

No-Churn Raspberry Sorbet

Beyond the basics...

Mash-ins

Scorched Honey, Fig and
Pecan Frozen Nougat

Rhubarb, Vanilla and
Almond Semi-Freddo

Watermelon and Mint Granita
with Lime Syrup

No-Churn Mango Sorbet

Frozen desserts

The basics...

Few of us own an ice cream machine,
but there's no need to worry –
plenty of delicious frozen desserts
can be made without one. In this
chapter I've included four different
techniques, including granitas, no-
churn sorbets, frozen nougat and
semi-freddo, some of which taste
like they have been through a churn!

Just like ice creams that have been
churned, all these desserts benefit
greatly from being frozen overnight,
so do your best to be organised and
reap the rewards.

And for those short on time (or
inclination), I've included a couple
of 'cheat's recipes'. But be warned,
they are so incredibly simple you
might be tempted not to bother with
anything else!

Peach and Champagne Granita

Okay, let's be honest, you don't have to be a kid to enjoy a slushie! Granita is really just a grown-up name for it, so here's one with grown-up ingredients too. It could be served as a refreshing end to a meal, but it could also be served as an alternative to pre-dinner drinks, particularly if it's a balmy summer's evening.

PREP TIME: *30 minutes*
COOKING TIME: *5 minutes*
FREEZING TIME: *4–5 hours*
MAKES: *4 serves*

750ML (3 CUPS) CHAMPAGNE

55G (¼ CUP) CASTER SUGAR

500G RIPE PEACHES (SEE NOTE)

1   Combine the champagne and sugar in a large saucepan over a medium-low heat, and stir, without boiling, until the sugar has dissolved. Increase the heat so that the champagne comes to a simmer, and simmer for 5 minutes. Take off the heat and cool completely. (To speed this up you can pour it into a stainless steel bowl that sits over another bowl of ice, and stir occasionally until it is cold. This takes about 5–10 minutes.)

2   Meanwhile, score a small cross in the skin at the base of each peach. Place into a heatproof bowl and cover with boiling water. Stand for 1 minute, then drain, cool slightly and slip off the skins. Remove the stones and place the flesh into a food processor. Process until very smooth. Add a little of the cooled champagne mixture to help it become even smoother.

3   Combine with the remaining champagne mixture. Pour through a sieve into a shallow cake tin (20cm x 20cm, or similar) and place into the freezer.

4   Freeze for about 4–5 hours, using a fork to scrape the mixture occasionally to help the crystals form, until firm.

5   Just prior to serving, scrape again with a fork as necessary to loosen the ice crystals.

NOTE

This recipe could be used as a base for other flavours. Try using strawberries instead of peaches, or, for a non-alcoholic tropical twist, replace the champagne with equal parts orange and pineapple juice, and the peaches for equal parts mango puree and passionfruit juice.

Rose, Raspberry and Pistachio Frozen Nougat

Frozen nougat uses a base of Swiss meringue and cream. Then any flavour can be added. Once frozen, it is smooth with a slightly chewy texture.

PREP TIME: *20 minutes*

COOKING TIME: *8–10 minutes*

FREEZING TIME: *4 hours minimum (preferably overnight)*

MAKES: *8 serves*

3 EGG WHITES

110G (½ CUP) CASTER SUGAR

200ML POURING CREAM

1 TSP ROSEWATER

150G RASPBERRIES, FRESH OR FROZEN

50G PISTACHIOS, CHOPPED

2 PUNNETS FRESH RASPBERRIES, EXTRA, TO SERVE

1   Spray a 22cm x 8cm (base measurement) loaf tin with oil spray, and line with baking paper, extending over the two long sides. Place into the freezer.

2   Place the egg whites and caster sugar into a heatproof bowl that fits snugly over a saucepan of gently simmering water (don't let the bottom of the bowl touch the water). Using electric hand beaters, whisk on low speed until the mixture has reached 65°C on a sugar thermometer. If you don't have a thermometer, it's the temperature where you can dip your finger in but you wouldn't want to leave it there!

3   Tip the egg-white mixture into the bowl of an electric stand mixer with a whisk attachment, and mix on high for about 3 minutes, until the mixture stops steaming. Reduce the speed to medium and continue mixing for another 3 minutes, until the mixture is just warm. Reduce the speed to low and continue whisking for another 3 minutes, until the mixture reaches room temperature. It should be so thick and glossy it's hard to resist putting your finger in for a lick!

4   In a separate bowl, whip the cream to soft peaks. Fold the whipped cream into the meringue mixture until well combined and then stir in the rosewater, raspberries and pistachios.

5   Pour the mixture into the prepared loaf tin and cover with plastic wrap. Freeze for a minimum of 4 hours, but preferably overnight, until firm.

6   Just before serving, invert onto a serving platter and remove the baking paper. Use a sharp knife to cut into thick slices and serve immediately, with fresh raspberries on the side.

NOTE

This recipe needs to be made the day before serving. It keeps in the freezer for up to 2 weeks.

Choc-Dipped Frozen Fruit on a Stick

Some years ago we regularly visited a Friday night food market where they served an eclectic mix of delicious food. I always finished the evening off with a piece of frozen fruit that had been dipped in chocolate. This is my version, and what I love most about it is that it's so simple!

PREP TIME: *10 minutes*
FREEZING TIME: *4 hours*
MAKES: *4–8*

2 LARGE MANGOES

8 ICY POLE STICKS

2 PUNNETS OF LARGE STRAWBERRIES

200G DARK CHOCOLATE

200G MILK CHOCOLATE

1   Line a baking tray with baking paper.

2   Peel each mango, using a small paring knife to remove all the skin. Cut off 2 large cheeks from each. Insert an icy pole stick two-thirds of the way into each mango cheek, ensuring it is centred so that it can support the weight of the mango. Place onto the baking tray.

3   Hull the strawberries and place 1 on each remaining icy pole stick. Place onto the baking tray with the mangoes and freeze until partially frozen (about 1 hour).

4   Roughly chop the chocolate and place into a small microwave-safe bowl (I like to use a jug for ease of dipping later), and microwave on high for 30 seconds. Stir the mixture and continue to microwave in 30-second bursts, stirring in between, until the chocolate is melted and smooth.

5   Working quickly, dip each stick of fruit into the chocolate, coating two-thirds of it. Place back onto the baking tray and refreeze for at least 4 hours before serving ... and then fight over who gets which one!

NOTE

These need to be made at least 4 hours before serving and will keep in the freezer for up to a week. Mango dipped in white chocolate works quite well too. For extra texture you could dip the chocolate-coated fruit into finely chopped nuts, coconut or sprinkles before the chocolate has set.

Individual Chocolate and Hazelnut Semi-Freddo

Semi-freddos are made from a cooked egg and sugar base (known as a sabayon), which is combined with cream and flavouring. Semi-freddos are a little icier than an ice cream, but they still make a creamy, luscious end to a meal.

PREP TIME: *25 minutes*
COOKING TIME: *10 minutes*
FREEZING TIME: *4 hours minimum (preferably overnight)*
MAKES: *16*

75G (½ CUP) HAZELNUTS

150G DARK CHOCOLATE, CHOPPED

100G CHOCOLATE HAZELNUT SPREAD

3 EGGS

2 EGG YOLKS

110G (½ CUP) CASTER SUGAR

430ML (1¾ CUPS) POURING CREAM

150G DARK CHOCOLATE, CHOPPED, EXTRA

150G MILK CHOCOLATE, CHOPPED

1 Spray 16 holes of large (½-cup capacity) muffin tins with oil spray, and line the base of each with a small round of baking paper.

2 Place the hazelnuts into a dry frying pan over a medium-low heat and cook, stirring occasionally, until they are golden and fragrant. Cool, then tip them into a clean tea towel and rub as much of their skins off as possible. Place the peeled hazelnuts into a food processor and process to medium-coarse crumbs.

3 Place the chocolate and chocolate hazelnut spread into a heatproof bowl that fits snugly over a saucepan of gently simmering water (don't let the bottom of the bowl touch the water). Stir until melted and smooth. Take the bowl off the heat and allow it to cool for 10 minutes while you prepare the egg mixture.

4 Combine the eggs, egg yolks and sugar in another heatproof bowl that fits snugly over a saucepan of gently simmering water (don't let the bottom of the bowl touch the water). Using electric hand beaters, whisk for 4–5 minutes until pale and thick. Remove from the heat and transfer to an electric stand mixer. Mix on low speed until the mixture has cooled to room temperature, or close to it.

5 Stir the chocolate mixture into the egg mixture. Add the chopped hazelnuts and stir to combine.

6 In a separate bowl, whip the cream to soft peaks. Fold the cream into the chocolate mixture until just combined.

7 Pour into the prepared muffin tins, filling each hole. Freeze for a minimum of 4 hours, but preferably overnight.

8 Just before serving, place the extra dark and the milk chocolate into a microwave-safe bowl. Microwave on high for 30 seconds and then stir. Continue to microwave in 30-second bursts, stirring in between, until all the chocolate is melted.

9 Run a knife around each semi-freddo and lever each one out. Place onto serving plates. Peel away the paper and pour a little melted chocolate over each.

NOTE

This recipe needs to be made the day before serving. It keeps in the freezer for up to 2 weeks.

No-Churn Raspberry Sorbet

Years ago, before I owned an ice cream machine, I discovered this method of making sorbet. It's so simple and so tasty. And it works with many different flavours – but unsurprisingly raspberry is my favourite!

PREP TIME: *30 minutes (in total)*
COOKING TIME: *10 minutes*
FREEZING TIME: *a couple of days*
MAKES: *750ml*

110G (½ CUP) CASTER SUGAR

180ML (¾ CUP) WATER

350G RASPBERRIES
(FRESH OR FROZEN)

JUICE OF ½ LIME

1 EGG WHITE

1 Combine the sugar and water in a small saucepan and stir over a medium-low heat, without boiling, until the sugar has dissolved. Increase the heat and bring to a simmer. Cook, without stirring, for a further minute. Cool the mixture to room temperature.

2 Put the sugar syrup, raspberries and lime juice into a blender and blend until smooth.

3 Pour through a sieve into a metal baking tray (18cm x 18cm x 4cm or similar), and freeze until solid (3 hours minimum, but preferably overnight).

4 Run a knife around the edge of the frozen raspberry mixture and cut it into large pieces that will fit in your food processor. Place the pieces into the processor with the egg white and process until smooth. Spoon back into the metal tray and re-freeze until firm (4 hours minimum, but preferably overnight).

5 Cut and scrape the mixture out, and place back into the food processor to blend until smooth once more. Refreeze in the same tin overnight before serving.

NOTE

This recipe is best made in stages over 3 days. Once it's ready, it keeps in the freezer for up to a week. It's helpful to know that homemade sorbets melt very quickly once out of the freezer, so eat quickly! If, after storing the gelato for a few days, it becomes icy again, simply process it once more and refreeze.

Beyond the basics...

Mash-Ins

As a child I loved to stir my toppings through my ice cream before I ate it. As I've got older it's progressed to slightly more decadent things! It remains one of our staple emergency dessert ideas. It is so simple that I often feel guilty that we're not putting in more effort – but it tastes so good that I soon get over that!

PREP TIME: *10–15 minutes*
FREEZING TIME: *1 hour*
MAKES: *8 serves*

1 LITRE GOOD-QUALITY
VANILLA ICE CREAM

200G PURCHASED CHOCOLATE
HONEYCOMB

1   Leave the ice cream out of the freezer for 10–15 minutes, until softened slightly.

2   Meanwhile, crush the chocolate honeycomb pieces. (I tend to wrap the pack in a tea towel and use the handle of a big knife to bash each piece through the packaging, which keeps it relatively contained.) They don't need to be a uniform size; in fact, I quite like having irregular sizing.

3   Stir the chocolate honeycomb into the ice cream and return it to the freezer for at least 1 hour.

NOTE

Use purchased vanilla ice cream, or see the ice cream chapter for recipes. We have explored so many variations using different ingredients. You are limited only by the flavours you like! Try these for equally good but different flavours: mint crisps, leftover chocolate brownie pieces, Maltesers, or, for the kids, Mini M&Ms.

Scorched Honey, Fig and Pecan Frozen Nougat

Scorched honey is a recent discovery of mine. I find that when honey is heated and cooked like a syrup for a few minutes, its flavour intensifies. It's perfect for using in this frozen nougat as the flavour holds up to freezing and the competition from the other ingredients.

PREP TIME: *40 minutes*
COOKING TIME: *15 minutes*
FREEZING TIME: *4 hours minimum (preferably overnight)*
MAKES: *8 serves*

120G (1 CUP) PECANS

125G GLACE FIGS

2½ TBS HONEY

3 EGG WHITES

110G (½ CUP) CASTER SUGAR

200ML POURING CREAM

1 Spray a 22cm x 8cm (base measurement) loaf tin with oil spray and line with baking paper, extending over the two long sides. Place into the freezer.

2 Toast the pecans. Chop the pecans and figs as finely as you can manage (the figs are a bit sticky!). They need to be small enough so that when the nougat is sliced it doesn't tear apart.

3 To scorch the honey, place it in a small saucepan over low heat, and heat until runny. Increase the heat to medium and then simmer until it has reduced to 1½ tablespoons. It will take a few minutes, depending on your stove.

4 Place the egg whites and caster sugar into a heatproof bowl that fits snugly over a saucepan of gently simmering water (don't let the bottom of the bowl touch the water). Using electric hand beaters, whisk on low speed until the mixture has reached 65°C on a sugar thermometer. If you don't have a thermometer, it's the temperature where you can dip your finger in but you wouldn't want to leave it there!

5 Add the warm scorched honey to the warm meringue and continue to beat for a further minute. It's important that both mixtures are warm so the honey doesn't crystallise in the mixture.

6 Tip the egg white mixture into the bowl of an electric stand mixer, with the whisk attachment, and mix on high for about 3 minutes, until the mixture stops steaming. Reduce the speed to medium and continue mixing for another 3 minutes, until the mixture is just warm. Reduce the speed to low and continue whisking for another 3 minutes, until the mixture reaches room temperature. It should be so thick and glossy it's hard to resist putting your finger in for a lick!

7 In a separate bowl, whip the cream to soft peaks. Fold the whipped cream into the meringue mixture until well combined and then fold in the chopped pecans and figs.

8 Pour the mixture into the prepared loaf tin and cover with plastic wrap. Freeze for a minimum of 4 hours, but preferably overnight, until firm. Cut into thick slices to serve.

Rhubarb, Vanilla and Almond Semi-Freddo

I'm a recent convert to rhubarb. I used to find the tart nature of it a little unsettling, but when it's in proper balance it's a fruit like no other, and I must confess I now love it. It seems to be very good friends with both vanilla and almond so this is a great combination.

PREP TIME: *20 minutes*
COOKING TIME: *8-10 minutes*
FREEZING TIME: *5 hours minimum (preferably overnight)*
MAKES: *6 serves*

300G RHUBARB, WASHED

100ML ORANGE JUICE

1 TBS CASTER SUGAR

4 EGG YOLKS

75G (⅓ CUP) CASTER SUGAR, EXTRA

1 VANILLA BEAN, SPLIT, SEEDS SCRAPED

300ML POURING CREAM

70G (½ CUP) SLIVERED ALMONDS, LIGHTLY TOASTED

1 Spray a 22cm x 8cm (base measurement) loaf tin with oil spray and line with baking paper, extending over the two long sides. Place into the freezer.

2 Trim the rhubarb and chop into 2cm pieces. Combine with the orange juice and caster sugar in a medium saucepan, and bring to a simmer. Cook for about 8–10 minutes over medium-high heat, stirring occasionally, until the rhubarb has collapsed and the liquid has become slightly syrupy. Transfer to a bowl to cool completely.

3 Combine the egg yolks, sugar and vanilla seeds in a heatproof bowl that fits snugly over a saucepan of gently simmering water (ensure that the water does not touch the bottom of the bowl). Use electric hand beaters to whisk until the mixture is thick and pale, and has reached about 85°C on a sugar thermometer (if you don't have a sugar thermometer, it should be too hot to leave your finger in there!).

4 Tip the mixture into the bowl of an electric stand mixer and beat on low speed until it has returned to room temperature.

5 In a separate bowl, whip the cream to soft peaks.

6 Fold together the cooled egg mixture and cream until combined thoroughly. Stir in the cooled rhubarb and toasted almonds.

7 Tip the mixture into the prepared loaf tin and cover with plastic wrap. Freeze for a minimum of 5 hours, but preferably overnight, until firm.

8 Allow the semi-freddo to soften slightly before scooping into serving bowls.

NOTE

This recipe needs to be made the day before serving. It keeps in the freezer for up to 2 weeks.

Watermelon and Mint Granita with Lime Syrup

My extended family has a shack in the Snowy Mountains. The kitchen is very basic with everyone's hand-me-downs, so when my kids asked on the day before we left (when food supplies were low) if they could cook dessert, we had to be creative. They decided to mash some watermelon with a fork, add some mint leaves and freeze it. I was dubious as to whether I would partake in this dessert but, being the dutiful mum, I did ... and proceeded to finish off the bowl, as it was delicious. That memorable moment has inspired this recipe – which happens to have just a little more technique!

PREP TIME: *15 minutes*
 (plus 45 minutes macerating time)
COOKING TIME: *5 minutes*
FREEZING TIME: *4–5 hours*
MAKES: *4 serves*

750G WATERMELON FLESH, ROUGHLY CHOPPED

55G (¼ CUP) CASTER SUGAR

10 MINT LEAVES, FINELY SHREDDED

250ML (1 CUP) WATER

220G (1 CUP) CASTER SUGAR, EXTRA

JUICE OF 2 LIMES

4 MINT LEAVES, FINELY SHREDDED, EXTRA

1 Put the watermelon into a bowl and sprinkle the sugar over it. Set aside for 45 minutes to macerate.

2 Place the watermelon into a food processor with the mint and process until smooth. Pour through a sieve into a shallow cake tin (20cm x 20cm, or similar), and place into the freezer.

3 Freeze for about 4–5 hours, using a fork to scrape the mixture occasionally to help the crystals form, until firm.

4 To make the lime syrup, combine the water and extra sugar in a small saucepan, and stir over low heat, without boiling, until the sugar has dissolved. Add the lime juice and increase the heat slightly. Simmer for 5 minutes. Take off the heat and cool completely.

5 To serve, spoon the granita into serving glasses and drizzle with lime syrup. Scatter with extra shredded mint leaves.

NOTE

This recipe is best made 5 hours before consuming. If kept longer, it will need to be re-scraped with a fork to break up the ice crystals.

No-Churn Mango Sorbet

We used to have a large mango tree in our backyard, and each summer we had more mangoes than we could give away! So I started making mango gelato, and soon there was no problem getting through the mangoes. This recipe uses a similar technique to the Raspberry Sorbet (page 130), but this one includes white wine, which gives an even silkier texture (interestingly, without adding the taste of wine).

PREP TIME: *30 minutes + chilling*
COOKING TIME: *10 minutes*
FREEZING TIME: *a couple of days*
MAKES: *750ml*

220G (1 CUP) CASTER SUGAR

250ML (1 CUP) WATER

250ML (1 CUP) DRY WHITE WINE

1 CUP (250 ML) MANGO PUREE

2 EGG WHITES

1 Combine the sugar, water and wine in a medium saucepan and stir over a medium-low heat, without boiling, until the sugar has dissolved.

2 Increase the heat so that the mixture just starts to bubble, and simmer for 10 minutes. Transfer to a bowl and cool to room temperature. (To speed this up you can pour it into a stainless steel bowl that sits over another bowl of ice and stir occasionally until it is cold. This takes about 20–30 minutes.)

3 Combine the cooled syrup with the mango puree and pour into a cake tin or similar metal container. Cover and freeze for about 3 hours, until solid.

4 Remove the solid mass from the cake tin and chop into chunks that fit into your food processor. Process the frozen pieces and egg whites until smooth. Pour back into the rinsed tin and refreeze for about 3 hours, until solid.

5 Process the mixture once more and refreeze a last time, preferably overnight, before serving.

NOTE

This recipe is best made in stages over 3 days. Once it's ready, it keeps in the freezer for up to a week. Homemade sorbets melt very quickly once out of the freezer – so eat quickly!

Gelatine

The basics...

When I was a child, jelly was the reason I wanted to have my tonsils out! There is something very lovable about something as simple as jelly. But gelatine can be used for so much more than just your standard jelly in a bowl. It is used in panna cottas, mousses, confectionery, and even in sauces to give them added body.

Gelatine comes in two main forms: powder and leaves. I use leaves, as I find them easier and completely flavourless. I generally use gold strength leaves (about 2g per leaf), but on occasion when a lot of gelatine is required I use titanium strength (about 5g per leaf), simply because it is more economical.

Gelatine leaves need to be soaked in cold water before they are used, and because there are no hard and fast rules of how many leaves will set how much liquid, it is best to stick to the recipe ... unless you're someone like me who actually likes experimenting (and is willing to wear the consequences!).

Strawberry Mousse (Maya's favourite)

In my opinion, everyone needs a dessert mousse in their repertoire. I love this one because it is fresh and fruity.

PREP TIME: *30 minutes*
COOKING TIME: *5–10 minutes*
REFRIGERATING TIME: *3 hours*
MAKES: *6 serves*

1½ GOLD-STRENGTH GELATINE LEAVES

2 EGG WHITES

110G (½ CUP) CASTER SUGAR

150ML POURING CREAM

250G STRAWBERRIES

JUICE OF ½ A LIME

1 Soak the gelatine leaves in a bowl of cold water for 5 minutes to soften.

2 Meanwhile, place the egg whites and sugar into a bowl that fits snugly over a saucepan of simmering water. Whisk the mixture continuously over the water (make sure it doesn't touch the bottom of the bowl) until it becomes the temperature of very hot water. (If you have a thermometer it should reach 65°C.) Squeeze the excess water from the softened gelatine leaves and add them to the egg whites, whisking for about 1 minute, until dissolved.

3 Tip the hot mixture into the bowl of an electric mixer with the whisk attachment and whisk on high until it stops steaming. Reduce the speed to medium and whisk until the mixture is just warm. Reduce the speed to low and whisk until the mixture is room temperature.

4 Meanwhile, in a separate bowl, whip the cream to soft peaks.

5 Place the strawberries and lime juice in a blender and blend until smooth. Strain through a sieve into a jug.

6 Beating on low speed, add the strawberry puree to the egg-white mixture. Fold in the cream and pour into six 150ml-capacity serving glasses. Refrigerate for about 3 hours, until set.

NOTE

This can be made ahead of time and stored in the fridge for up to 3 days.

Blackcurrant Jelly

I have enjoyed the flavour of blackcurrant since I was a child, thanks to cordial, so consider this my tribute to Ribena. Serve it in little glasses to the children in your life and enjoy a trip down memory lane yourself.

PREP TIME: *5 minutes*
COOKING TIME: *5 minutes*
REFRIGERATING TIME: *4 hours minimum (preferably overnight)*
MAKES: *4 serves*

4 GOLD-STRENGTH GELATINE LEAVES

90ML RIBENA FRUIT JUICE SYRUP

410ML WATER

1 Soak the gelatine leaves in cold water for 5 minutes until softened.

2 Meanwhile, place the Ribena and water into a medium saucepan and bring to a simmer. Take the saucepan off the heat. Squeeze the excess water from the gelatine leaves, and add to the pan. Stir until the gelatine has dissolved.

3 Pour the mixture through a strainer into a jug, then pour into four 125ml (½ cup capacity) serving glasses.

4 Refrigerate for about 4 hours, or overnight, until set.

NOTE

This can be made ahead of time and kept in the fridge for up to 1 week.

Earl Grey Panna Cotta

These cute little panna cottas are so easy to make, especially because there is no need to turn them out (and therefore no risk of them collapsing). But beware of the surprise – they may look like a warm cup of Earl Grey tea but they are a cold dessert. Sometimes it's fun to play tricks!

PREP TIME: *15 minutes*
COOKING TIME: *5 minutes*
REFRIGERATING TIME: *4 hours minimum (preferably overnight)*
MAKES: *4 serves*

600ML POURING CREAM

55G (¼ CUP) CASTER SUGAR

2 TSP EARL GREY TEA LEAVES

3½ GOLD-STRENGTH GELATINE LEAVES

FEW DROPS OF PARISIAN ESSENCE, OPTIONAL

4 AMARETTI BISCUITS, TO SERVE (SEE NOTE)

1 Place the cream, sugar and tea leaves in a medium saucepan over medium heat. Heat, stirring occasionally, until steaming. Take off the heat and allow the tea to infuse for 15 minutes. Pour the cream through a fine sieve (a tea strainer works well!) to strain off the tea leaves.

2 Soak the gelatine leaves in a bowl of cold water for 5 minutes to soften.

3 Rinse out the saucepan, return the cream mixture to the saucepan and reheat until steaming again.

4 Take the pan off the heat. Squeeze excess water from the gelatine leaves and add to the pan. Stir until the gelatine is dissolved. Add a few drops of Parisian essence, if using, to bring it to the colour of a milky cup of tea.

5 Strain the mixture again and then divide evenly among 4 old-style teacups.

6 Refrigerate for about 4 hours, or overnight, until set.

7 Serve the teacup of panna cotta on its saucer, with an amaretti biscuit on the side.

NOTE

These panna cottas need to be made ahead of time and can be kept in the fridge for up to 3 days. They can be set in lightly oiled dariole moulds, and then turned out onto serving plates. To turn out of the moulds, gently ease one section of the top edge away from the mould and tease it back to let an air bubble make its way to the base. Then place a plate over the mould, invert and let it gently fall out. Use purchased amaretti biscuits, or see page 235 for my recipe.

Beyond the basics...

ᵧᵧᵧ Turkish Delight

I'm not one who usually tries to make my own confectionery, but I do have a soft spot for Turkish Delight and I get a great sense of satisfaction when I look at my homemade batch of it.

PREP TIME: *30 minutes*
COOKING TIME: *90 minutes*
REFRIGERATING TIME: *overnight*
MAKES: *36 pieces*

880G (4 CUPS) CASTER SUGAR

1L (4 CUPS) WATER

2 TBS LEMON JUICE

150G (1 CUP) CORNFLOUR

1 TSP CREAM OF TARTAR

2 TSP ROSEWATER

FEW DROPS OF RED FOOD COLOURING

4½ TITANIUM-STRENGTH GELATINE LEAVES (SEE NOTE)

320G (2 CUPS) ICING SUGAR MIXTURE

1   Spray an 18cm square cake tin with oil, and line the base and sides with baking paper. Oil the paper as well.

2   Place the sugar and 500ml (2 cups) of the water into a large saucepan. Stir over medium-low heat until the sugar has dissolved. Increase the heat and bring to a simmer.

3   Cook without stirring for 50–60 minutes, brushing down the sides of the pan regularly with a very wet pastry brush to remove any crystals, until the mixture reaches 125°C on a sugar thermometer. If you don't have a sugar thermometer, drop a little syrup into a glass of cold water and it should form a thick rope. When completely cooled it will be hard and brittle. Take it off the heat and stir in the lemon juice.

4   Place the cornflour and cream of tartar into another saucepan. Add a little of the remaining 500ml (2 cups) of water and stir to form a paste. Gradually add the remaining water, stirring in well to avoid lumps. If at any stage you do get lumps it is worth straining them out or you end up with hard lumps in the finished product. Cook over medium heat, whisking constantly, until the mixture thickens.

5   Gradually pour the sugar syrup into the cornflour mixture, whisking constantly. Bring to a simmer and cook gently, stirring regularly, for a further 5 minutes. It will look a bit like glue at this stage! Add the rosewater and food colouring and mix until combined.

6   Meanwhile, soak the gelatine leaves in cold water for 5 minutes until they have softened. Squeeze the excess water from the leaves, and add to the pan. Stir until dissolved.

7   Pour into the prepared tin. Set aside to cool to room temperature, then refrigerate overnight until set.

8   When ready to serve, pour the icing sugar mixture onto a large chopping board. Turn the Turkish Delight onto the sugar and, using a lightly greased knife, cut it into 3cm square pieces. Toss the pieces in the icing sugar mixture to coat thoroughly then place on a plate to serve.

NOTE

This can be made ahead of time (up to the end of step 7) and will keep well in an airtight container for up to 1 week. It is best to cut and roll it in icing sugar just prior to serving. Because this recipe needs a lot of gelatine, I use titanium strength.

Plum and Red Wine Mousse

There is something beautiful about plum and red wine together. I absolutely love this combination, and in a creamy mousse it's one dessert I can just keep on eating (though I probably shouldn't!).

PREP TIME: *30 minutes*
COOKING TIME: *20 minutes*
REFRIGERATING TIME: *3 hours*
MAKES: *6 serves*

400G PLUMS, PITTED (SEE NOTE)

1 TBS CASTER SUGAR

60ML (¼ CUP) RED WINE

2 GOLD-STRENGTH GELATINE LEAVES

2 EGG WHITES

110G (½ CUP) CASTER SUGAR, EXTRA

150ML POURING CREAM

120G (½ CUP) SOUR CREAM

1 Combine the plums, caster sugar and red wine in a small saucepan. Bring to a simmer and cook over medium heat for about 10 minutes, until soft and thick. Cool slightly, and then place in a blender and blend until smooth. Pour through a sieve into a jug and set aside.

2 Soak the gelatine leaves in a bowl of cold water for 5 minutes to soften.

3 Meanwhile, place the egg whites and extra caster sugar into a bowl that fits snugly above a saucepan of simmering water. Whisk the mixture constantly over the water (make sure it doesn't touch the bottom of the bowl) until it has reached 65°C on a sugar thermometer. If you don't have a thermometer it's the temperature where you can dip your finger in but you wouldn't want to leave it there!

4 Squeeze the excess water from the gelatine leaves and add to the bowl. Whisk for about 1 minute, until dissolved.

5 Tip the hot mixture into the bowl of an electric mixer with the whisk attachment and whisk on high until it stops steaming. Reduce the speed to medium and whisk until the mixture is just warm. Reduce the speed to low and whisk until the mixture is room temperature.

6 Meanwhile, whip the cream to soft peaks. Add the sour cream and continue to mix until the soft peaks re-form.

7 Reserve 2 tablespoons of the plum puree. Add the rest to the egg-white mixture and mix thoroughly. Fold in the cream mixture and then pour it all into six 150ml-capacity serving glasses. Drizzle a teaspoon of the reserved plum puree over the top of each, and then refrigerate for about 3 hours, until set.

NOTE

This can be made ahead of time and stored in the fridge for up to 3 days. You can substitute tinned plums for the fresh ones – you'll probably need an 825g tin to get enough weight in drained plums.

Mango Panna Cotta with Orange Blossom Jelly

It's long been known that orange and mango go together, but here I've taken it just a little step further and added orange blossom to the mix. This dish can be a bit fiddly and time-consuming, but it looks so pretty when it's finished that you'll be really proud of yourself for pulling it off!

PREP TIME: *30 minutes*
COOKING TIME: *60 minutes*
REFRIGERATING TIME: *3 hours + overnight*
MAKES: *8 slices*

PANNA COTTA LAYER

6 GOLD-STRENGTH GELATINE LEAVES

600ML THICKENED CREAM

400ML MANGO PUREE (FROM 4 SMALL MANGOES)

FINELY GRATED ZEST OF 1 ORANGE

JELLY LAYER

5 GOLD-STRENGTH GELATINE LEAVES

110G (½ CUP) CASTER SUGAR

250ML (1 CUP) WATER

250ML (1 CUP) ORANGE JUICE (SEE NOTE)

1 TSP ORANGE BLOSSOM WATER

2 ORANGES, PEELED AND SEGMENTED

1 MANGO, PEELED AND DICED

1 For this dessert you will need a round 20cm (6cm deep) dessert ring (see note). Using a double layer of aluminium foil, create a collar which extends 3cm past the bottom edge of the ring and folds inwards to tuck under the ring when it is placed on the serving plate. This will stop the unset panna cotta from leaking out of the base of the ring too much but can be easily removed once the panna cotta is set and the ring removed.

2 For the panna cotta layer, soak the gelatine leaves in a bowl of cold water for 5 minutes to soften. Heat the cream over medium-low heat until steaming, stirring occasionally. Take the pan off the heat. Squeeze the excess water from the gelatine leaves and add to the cream, stirring until completely dissolved. Cool the mixture for about 15 minutes, until just above room temperature, and then stir in the mango puree and orange zest. Carefully pour into the dessert ring. Refrigerate for at least 3 hours, until set.

3 To prepare the jelly layer, soak the gelatine leaves in a bowl of cold water for 5 minutes to soften. Combine the sugar and water in a medium saucepan and stir over low heat until the sugar has dissolved. Add the orange juice and bring the mixture up to steaming point. Take the pan off the heat and add the orange blossom water. Squeeze the gelatine leaves to extract as much water as possible, then add to the hot liquid. Stir until the gelatine is fully dissolved. Pour the hot mixture through a sieve into a jug and then cool to room temperature.

4 Carefully pour the jelly onto the set panna cotta. Lower in the orange and mango pieces and then refrigerate overnight.

5 When ready to serve, place a hot, wet tea towel around the ring to loosen the panna cotta and jelly slightly from the sides of the ring. Carefully lift the ring off and gently pull the foil collar out from underneath.

NOTE

This recipe is best made the day before serving and will keep for up to 1 week in the fridge. If using freshly squeezed orange juice you will need to pour it through a sieve lined with muslin (or a new Chux) to prevent your jelly from being too cloudy. Dessert rings are bottomless rings available from specialist cooking shops. As an alternative you can use a springform tin, but the base will need to stay in place when you serve the panna cotta as removing it will be too difficult.

Pastry

The basics...

Pastry is such a satisfying thing to make, and the feeling of delight when you taste your own homemade version is like nothing else. It's true that lots of different factors come into play when making pastry, which is why it's ultimately made by feel! But these few tips should help:

- If the mixture is a bit on the dry side, add a little more liquid. If it's a bit on the wet side, add a bit more flour.

- Work your pastry minimally. As soon as it has come together and is smooth to the touch, stop playing with it!

- Always allow pastry to rest, otherwise it can be tough and shrink in the tin once it's cooked.

- Some pastry needs to be 'blind baked' before you add the filling. This simply means that the pastry is cooked but not browned. To prevent it from browning it is covered with baking paper and to prevent it from puffing up it is weighed down with baking weights. I use a stash of rice over and over again as my baking weights. If pastry is not blind baked it will rarely cook through properly. Follow the instructions in each recipe to see how simple it is.

Sweet Shortcrust Pastry

Sure, you can buy a shortcrust pastry from your local supermarket, but then you miss out on the satisfaction that comes from making your own. Not to mention the far superior taste and texture. Really, it's not as difficult as you think.

PREP TIME: *10 minutes*
RESTING TIME: *30 minutes*
MAKES: *530g pastry*

125G BUTTER,
CHILLED AND CUBED

110G (⅔ CUP) ICING SUGAR

250G (1⅔ CUPS)
PLAIN FLOUR, SIFTED

2 EGG YOLKS

1–2 TBS MILK

1 Place the butter and icing sugar in the bowl of a food processor and blend until creamed and smooth.

2 Add the flour and egg yolks. Using the pulse button on your food processor, process in short bursts until the mixture looks like coarse breadcrumbs.

3 Add 1 tablespoon of the milk, and, using the pulse button again, process in short bursts until the mixture is just starting to come together. Only use the second tablespoon of milk if you need it.

4 Tip the mixture out onto a lightly floured bench and knead minimally until it's smooth, then flatten it into a disc about 12cm in diameter.

5 Wrap tightly in plastic wrap and refrigerate for 30 minutes.

6 The pastry is now ready to be rolled out and blind baked for use in another application.

NOTE

This can be made ahead of time and stored, uncooked, in the freezer, for up to 3 months. A cooked tart case is best used the same day but can be kept in an airtight container for up to 2 days.

Maggie Beer's Sour Cream Pastry

Maggie Beer has one of the best pastry recipes I know because it is so simple but so buttery and flaky. I was thrilled therefore when she agreed to let me use it in my book. When you taste it, you'll hardly believe you made it yourself!

PREP TIME: *10 minutes*
RESTING TIME: *20 minutes*
MAKES: *550g pastry*

250G (1⅔ CUPS)
PLAIN FLOUR, SIFTED

200G BUTTER,
CHILLED AND CUBED

120ML (½ CUP) SOUR CREAM,
APPROXIMATELY

1 Place the flour and butter into a food processor, and, using the pulse button, process in short bursts until the mixture resembles coarse breadcrumbs.

2 Add about two-thirds of the sour cream. Using the pulse button, process in short bursts until it is just combined. Pinch a little of the dough in your fingers. If it holds together, it is ready. If it is still too dry and crumbly to hold together, add a little more sour cream and process again.

3 Tip the mixture out onto a lightly floured bench and gather together, pressing lightly until it's smooth, then flatten it into a disc about 12cm in diameter.

4 Wrap tightly in plastic wrap and refrigerate for 20 minutes.

5 The pastry is now ready to be rolled out and blind baked for use in another application.

NOTE

This pastry can be made ahead of time and stored in the fridge for up to 2 days, or in the freezer for up to 3 months.

Rough Puff Pastry

Rough Puff Pastry is really a cheat's version of Puff Pastry. It gives beautifully buttery results with a lot less effort. It is not a difficult procedure at all, but it is time-consuming, so do it when you're in the kitchen doing other things.

When cutting Puff Pastry, it's best to cut in sharp, downward cuts rather than dragging your knife through it, otherwise all the layers you have put into it will stick together and won't puff up very well.

PREP TIME: *45 minutes*
 + plus lots of resting
MAKES: *500g pastry (see Note)*

250G (1⅔ CUPS) PLAIN FLOUR, SIFTED

250G BUTTER, CHILLED AND CUBED

80ML (⅓ CUP) ICED WATER

1 Place the flour into a large, wide bowl if you have one (otherwise straight onto the bench). Place the butter cubes into the bowl with the flour and mix to coat the butter in the flour.

2 Make a well in the centre and add the iced water. Using a pastry scraper or firm spatula, mix to combine (it looks like a bit of a mess at this point).

3 Using your hands, gently gather the dough together. We are aiming to get it all together into a ball, but the ball will have lumps of butter in it. It should only take about a minute. Once it's come together, form it into a fat square about 3cm thick.

4 Wrap tightly in plastic wrap and place into the fridge for 30 minutes until firm.

5 Lightly flour your bench and rolling pin. Place the pastry onto the floured bench and roll into a rectangle about 1.5cm thick and about 15cm x 40cm. Don't worry about any remaining lumps of butter – they will eventually be worked out. We don't want to overwork the pastry too much at this stage. Fold the short ends in to meet at the centre.

6 Fold in half again to make a 'book' shape. Lightly push a finger into the corner to create a mark (this will be the way you keep track of how many times you've rolled it!). Wrap in plastic again and refrigerate for another 30 minutes.

7 Roll the pastry out again on the lightly floured bench to a similar size. Fold in the same way and then mark with two fingers in the corner (to indicate it's been rolled twice). Wrap again and refrigerate for another 30 minutes.

8 Repeat 2 more times so that it has been rolled and folded 4 times (the last time, don't put your finger marks on it or they will be there in the finished product).

9 It is now ready to roll out for use or store for later use in the fridge or freezer.

NOTE

Pastry can be made ahead of time and kept wrapped tightly in the fridge for up to 2 days, or in the freezer for up to 3 months. This is more pastry than you will usually need, but because it's a time-consuming process I like to make this amount and freeze the remainder for another time.

Beyond the basics...

Blueberry Frangipane Tart

I am blessed enough to have blueberries growing in my garden. They are such a versatile fruit, great in muffins, cakes, jams and ice creams, among many other things. Here, I've used them in a classic frangipane tart, which is one of my favourite ways to eat them.

PREP TIME: *25 minutes + 20 minutes resting*
COOKING TIME: *60 minutes*
MAKES: *6–8 slices*

½ QUANTITY OF SOUR CREAM PASTRY (SEE PAGE 167)

1 TBS SLIVERED ALMONDS

60G BUTTER

75G (⅓ CUP) CASTER SUGAR

1 EGG

1 TBS BRANDY

FINELY GRATED ZEST OF ¼ LEMON

100G ALMOND MEAL

3 TSP PLAIN FLOUR

250G FRESH BLUEBERRIES

TOASTED ALMONDS, FOR SCATTERING

THICK DOUBLE CREAM, TO SERVE

1 Preheat the oven to 175°C and lightly grease a 33cm x 12cm (base measurement) rectangular, loose-bottom fluted tart tin.

2 Roll the pastry out on a lightly floured bench, in a rectangle shape about 3mm thick, large enough to fit the tin. Lift from the edges regularly to ensure the pastry doesn't stick to the work surface (and add more flour if it's looking or feeling like it will!). Lay it carefully into the prepared tin, pressing to fit, and trim the edges. Refrigerate for 20 minutes.

3 Place the slivered almonds into a dry frying pan over a medium-low heat and cook, stirring occasionally, until they are golden and fragrant.

4 To blind bake the pastry, line with a large piece of baking paper, and fill with baking weights, or dried beans or rice. Bake for 10 minutes, then remove the paper and weights and bake for a further 10 minutes, until cooked through (it will feel dry and be an even colour). Set aside to cool.

5 For the frangipane, cream the butter and sugar in the bowl of an electric mixer until pale and creamy, scraping down the bowl as necessary. Add the egg, and mix to combine for 1 minute. Mix in the brandy and zest. Add the almond meal and flour, and mix until just combined.

6 Spread the almond mixture into the pastry case, taking care not to tear the delicate pastry. Top with blueberries in a single layer, and scatter with toasted almonds. Bake for 40 minutes, until golden brown.

7 Leave to cool in the tin. Remove from the tin and serve at room temperature, with thick double cream.

NOTE

This is best made the day of serving, but will keep in an airtight container for up to 3 days. For different flavours, you can easily substitute the blueberries for other berries. Peaches or nectarines would work nicely too.

Apricot and Thyme Tarte Tatin

Tarte Tatin is simply a fancy name for a French upside-down fruit tart, made in a frying pan and finished in the oven. In this recipe I've combined apricot and thyme, which is an unexpected but delicious combination.

PREP TIME: *20 minutes*
COOKING TIME: *50 minutes*
MAKES: *8–10 slices*

½ QUANTITY ROUGH PUFF
PASTRY (PAGE 168)

50G BUTTER

2 TBS CASTER SUGAR

1 TBS WATER

1 TSP LEMON JUICE

2 TSP THYME LEAVES,
PICKED FROM THE SPRIG

800G APRICOTS,
HALVED AND STONED

EXTRA THYME LEAVES, TO SERVE

THICK DOUBLE CREAM, TO SERVE

1 Preheat the oven to 200°C.

2 Roll the pastry out to a thickness of 3–4mm. Cut out a 26cm circle (I trace the frying pan I am going to use). Place onto a plate or board lined with baking paper, and cover with plastic wrap until needed.

3 Melt the butter in a 26cm (top measurement) ovenproof frying pan over medium heat. Add the sugar and stir to combine. Add the water and lemon juice and stir until the sugar has dissolved. Bring to a simmer and cook gently for 3–5 minutes, or until the sugar has begun to caramelise and is the colour of honey. Remove from the heat.

4 Sprinkle the thyme leaves over, and then arrange the apricot halves into the pan, cut side up. Ensure they are in a single layer and that the base of the frying pan is completely covered. Lay the pastry over the top of the fruit, tucking the edges down around the apricots.

5 Place into the oven and bake for 40 minutes, until the pastry is deeply golden and cooked through. Beware not to take the puff pastry out of the oven too early!

6 Allow the tart to sit for 2–3 minutes. Invert a serving plate over the top of the frying pan. Holding the plate securely, use a swift action to flip the frying pan so the tart turns out onto the plate. Scatter extra thyme leaves over the top and serve with double cream on the side.

NOTE

You could use purchased puff pastry if you like – I would choose the Careme brand. It is available from some supermarkets, or specialty food shops. If apricots are not in season, use an 825g can of apricot halves. Rinse briefly to rid them of the strong 'canned' flavour, then drain well and pat dry with paper towels.

Classic Lemon Tart

One of my all-time favourite desserts is this one. The flavours are simple and balanced, the pastry is thin and short, and the filling is creamy and yet refreshing. It ticks all the boxes for me!

PREP TIME: *20 minutes + 30 minutes resting*
COOKING TIME: *60 minutes*
REFRIGERATING TIME: *1 hour minimum (preferably overnight)*
MAKES: *8–10 slices*

1 QUANTITY OF SWEET SHORTCRUST PASTRY (SEE PAGE 166)

1 EGG WHITE, LIGHTLY WHISKED

4 EGGS

165G (¾ CUP) CASTER SUGAR

180ML (¾ CUP) DOUBLE CREAM

150ML FRESH LEMON JUICE (2–3 LEMONS)

FINELY GRATED ZEST OF 1 LEMON

ICING SUGAR, TO DUST

THICK DOUBLE CREAM, TO SERVE

1 PUNNET (ABOUT 125G) OF FRESH BLUEBERRIES, TO SERVE

1 Place the pastry onto a lightly floured bench top and roll out to a thickness of 3–4mm, to fit a 24cm (base measurement), loose-bottom fluted tart tin. Lift the pastry regularly to check that it's not sticking to the bench (and add more flour if it's looking or feeling like it will!). Carefully roll the pastry onto the rolling pin and gently 'unroll' the pastry into the tin. Gently press the pastry into the tin, and trim the edges, discarding any leftover pastry. Cover the tin with plastic wrap and return to the fridge for 30 minutes.

2 Preheat the oven to 170°C.

3 To blind bake the pastry, line it with a large piece of baking paper, and fill with baking weights, or dried beans or rice. Bake for 10 minutes, then remove the paper and weights and bake for a further 10 minutes, until cooked through (it will feel dry and be an even colour).

4 Remove the pastry from the oven and drop the oven temperature to 150°C. Using a pastry brush, brush a thin film of egg white all over the inside of the pastry case.

5 To make the filling, whisk the eggs and sugar in a medium bowl until pale and slightly thickened. Stir in the cream, juice and zest. Allow it to sit for a few minutes and then skim off any foam that has risen to the top, and discard.

6 Pour the lemon filling into the case. (I find that if I leave the pastry case in the oven I am less likely to spill it in transit!) Bake for 40 minutes, until the filling is set on the surface with a slight wobble underneath.

7 Cool to room temperature, then refrigerate for at least 1 hour, but preferably overnight, before serving.

8 Dust with icing sugar, cut into wedges and serve with thick double cream and blueberries.

NOTE

This recipe can be made ahead of time and will keep in the fridge for up to a week. Some or all of the lemon juice could be substituted for lime and/or orange juice to create other beautifully zesty flavours. For something different try ruby red grapefruit.

Pear, Walnut and Mascarpone Galette

There's something special about the combination of pear, walnut and mascarpone. Whether they are sitting together on a cheese platter or in a dessert, it's obvious that they're the very best of friends!

PREP TIME: *30 minutes*
COOKING TIME: *30 minutes*
MAKES: *6–8 slices*

½ QUANTITY ROUGH PUFF PASTRY (SEE PAGE 168)

200G MASCARPONE

½ TSP GROUND CINNAMON

25G (¼ CUP) WALNUT PIECES

125ML (½ CUP) MAPLE SYRUP

4 FIRM PEARS

2 TBS BROWN SUGAR

30G BUTTER, CHOPPED

1 Preheat the oven to 190°C, and line a baking tray with baking paper.

2 To prepare the pastry, place it on a lightly floured bench top and roll out to a large rectangle about 3–4 mm thick. Lift at times to check that it's not sticking to the bench (and add more flour if it's looking or feeling like it will!). Cut and trim the pastry to create 2 neat rectangles, 20cm x 12cm each. Place onto the baking tray. Using the tip of a sharp knife score a 'frame' around the pastry, 2cm in from the edge. Make the cut about halfway into the thickness of the pastry.

3 For the mascarpone, combine it with the cinnamon, and stir until smooth and spreadable. Spread 1 tablespoon onto each pastry sheet inside the border. Reserve the remainder for serving with the galette.

4 To prepare the walnuts, place them into a dry frying pan over a medium-low heat. Cook for about 5 minutes, stirring occasionally, until they are slightly coloured and fragrant. Pour in the maple syrup and increase the heat to medium-high. Simmer for 2–3 minutes, until the syrup has reduced and become a little thicker. Set aside to cool slightly.

5 Peel the pears and cut lengthways into 2–3mm slices, using a mandolin (or sharp knife if you don't have a mandolin). Discard the core section. Fan the pear slices evenly over the mascarpone.

6 To finish, sprinkle the pear with the brown sugar and dot randomly with butter. Spoon the walnuts over, and drizzle with a little of the maple syrup reduction. Keep the remaining syrup for drizzling over after baking.

7 Bake for 30 minutes until the pastry is puffed and deeply golden. Just before serving, gently reheat the syrup reduction if necessary to bring it back to pouring consistency.

8 Top the tart with small dollops of the remaining mascarpone mixture, and drizzle with syrup just before serving.

NOTE

You could use purchased puff pastry if you like – I would choose the Careme brand. It is available from some supermarkets, or specialty food shops. You can also swap the fruit and nut combination around. Try apple and macadamia, or nectarine and slivered almonds.

White Chocolate and Rose Tartlets (Erin's favourite)

These sweet little tartlets are a bit too more-ish for my liking! I deliberately make them small because they are rich, but I usually end up eating two anyway. I just love the combination of white chocolate and rose. Serve them as a special afternoon tea treat, or with a pile of fresh berries for dessert.

PREP TIME: *15 minutes + 30 minutes resting*
COOKING TIME: *15–20 minutes*
REFRIGERATING TIME: *2 hours minimum (preferably overnight)*
MAKES: *12*

1 QUANTITY OF SWEET SHORTCRUST PASTRY (SEE PAGE 166)

400G GOOD-QUALITY WHITE CHOCOLATE, CHOPPED

160ML (⅔ CUP) POURING CREAM

½ TSP ROSEWATER

ICING SUGAR AND EDIBLE ROSEBUDS, TO GARNISH (SEE NOTE)

1   Lightly grease 12 holes of large (½-cup capacity) muffin tins.

2   Place the pastry onto a lightly floured bench top and roll out to 3mm thick. Using a 9cm round cutter, cut 12 rounds out of the pastry and ease into each muffin hole. Prick the base with a fork and refrigerate for 30 minutes.

3   Preheat the oven to 170°C.

4   To blind bake, line each pastry shell with a piece of baking paper, and fill with baking weights, or dried beans or rice. Screw the top of the paper together to create little 'money bags' so the weights are less likely to spill. Bake for 10 minutes, then remove the paper and weights and bake for a further 5–10 minutes, until cooked through (it will feel dry and be an even colour). Cool slightly and then transfer the tart shells to a wire rack to cool completely.

5   Meanwhile, combine the white chocolate, cream and rosewater in a microwave-safe bowl. Microwave on high for 30 seconds and then stir. Continue to microwave in 30-second bursts, stirring between each, until it is all melted and smooth when stirred. Taste for the rosewater – you may need to add more if you cannot detect it (different brands of rosewater have different potency).

6   Spoon the filling into the cooled tart shells. Refrigerate for about 2 hours, until set. Serve either chilled, or at room temperature, and garnish with a light dusting of icing sugar and edible rosebuds.

NOTE

These can be made ahead of time and stored in an airtight container for up to 1 week. Edible rosebuds are available from specialist and Middle Eastern food shops. For an even simpler process you can purchase pre-made pastry cases, but in my humble opinion they're never quite as good as the homemade version! Vary the recipe to make Jaffa Tarts – simply replace the white chocolate with dark chocolate and use finely grated orange zest instead of rosewater.

Embarrassingly Simple Chocolate Hazelnut Pastries

It was one of those moments when I had some scraps of Puff Pastry left over (and a few extra minutes), so I decided to use them rather than throw them out, knowing that my kids would lap them up for afternoon tea. The result was so good I made them again when friends were coming round for afternoon tea the following day. They loved them as well, but I was too embarrassed to tell them how simple they were to make!

PREP TIME: *10 minutes*
COOKING TIME: *20 minutes*
MAKES: *8 serves*

½ QUANTITY ROUGH PUFF
PASTRY (SEE PAGE 168)

1 EGG, LIGHTLY BEATEN

3 TBS CHOCOLATE HAZELNUT
SPREAD

ICING SUGAR, TO DUST

1 Preheat the oven to 200°C, and line a baking tray with baking paper.

2 Roll the pastry on a lightly floured surface to a rectangle about 3–4 mm thick. Trim the edges and then cut the pastry into eight evenly-sized squares, about 8cm x 8cm.

3 Brush each square with the beaten egg. Put 1½ teaspoons of chocolate hazelnut spread just off-centre of each square and spread it slightly into a triangular shape. Fold the pastry in half over the top to create a triangle. Press the pastry together at the edges, ensuring they are sealed well. Brush the top of each pastry triangle with egg.

4 Bake for 20 minutes, until the pastry is deeply golden and puffed. Cool slightly, then dust liberally with icing sugar.

NOTE

You could use purchased Puff Pastry if you like – I would choose the Careme brand. It is available from some supermarkets, or specialty food shops.

♈♈♈ Old-Fashioned Apple Pie

This is a hearty dessert so I've made it a hearty size! Feel free to downsize to suit your needs but whatever you do make sure you serve it with crème anglaise (see page 62), cream or ice cream (or if you're like my dad, serve it with all three!).

PREP TIME: *60 minutes*
COOKING TIME: *60–65 minutes*
MAKES: *10–12 slices*

1KG GRANNY SMITH APPLES

2 TBS LEMON JUICE

60G BUTTER

2 TBS BROWN SUGAR

2 TSP VANILLA EXTRACT

1 QUANTITY OF SOUR CREAM
PASTRY (SEE PAGE 167)

30G (¼ CUP) ALMOND MEAL

2 TBS FLAKED ALMONDS

1 EGG, LIGHTLY BEATEN

1 TBS WHITE SUGAR

CRÈME ANGLAISE (SEE PAGE 62),
THICK DOUBLE CREAM AND/OR
A GOOD-QUALITY VANILLA ICE
CREAM, TO SERVE

1 Preheat the oven to 180°C. Lightly grease a 21cm (base measurement), 5cm deep, fluted tart tin (or dish of a similar size).

2 Peel and core the apples, and dice into cubes about 1.5cm x 1.5cm. As you prepare them, place them into a large bowl with the lemon juice and toss to coat (this prevents them from browning).

3 Melt the butter in a large saucepan over a medium heat. Stir in the sugar and vanilla and then add the apples. Stir to coat the apples in the butter. Cook over a medium heat for 5–10 minutes, stirring occasionally, until just tender. Transfer to a wide bowl and cool to room temperature.

4 Meanwhile, roll two-thirds of the sour cream pastry on a floured work surface to a thickness of 3–4mm. Line the prepared tin, pressing down as necessary. Trim the edges.

5 To blind bake the pastry, line with a large piece of baking paper, and fill with baking weights, or dried beans or rice. Bake for 10 minutes, then remove the paper and weights and bake for a further 10 minutes, until cooked through (it will feel dry and be an even colour).

6 Sprinkle the almond meal over the pastry base. Fill with half the apple mixture. Sprinkle with the flaked almonds, then spread the remaining apples over. It may need mounding lightly in the middle to fit it all in.

7 Roll the remaining pastry on a floured work surface to a thickness of 3–4mm.

8 Brush the edges of the cooked pastry with a little beaten egg, then lay the freshly rolled pastry on the top of the apples. Press very lightly onto the pastry edge, and trim any excess from around the top of the tin. Remember, apple pies are meant to be rustic-looking!

9 Brush the top of the pie with more egg, and pierce the centre of the pie with the tip of a small sharp knife, to allow steam to escape. Sprinkle with the white sugar. Bake for 35–40 minutes, until the pastry is deeply golden. Serve with crème anglaise, thick double cream and ice cream!

NOTE

This is best eaten straight out of the oven, but will keep in an airtight container for 3 days. If keeping, gently warm before serving.

Cakes & puddings

The basics...

When it comes to cooking, cake baking was my first love. One of the beautiful things about cakes is that they come in so many different forms and flavours. I've taken four very basic cake-making techniques as a starting point: traditional cakes, melt-and-mix cakes, flourless cakes and puddings. However, there are so many other options out there.

When baking cakes, remember that ovens, ingredients and equipment vary slightly, so use the recipe as a guide, but also remember that you have the final say.

Generally speaking, I use the middle shelf of the oven for baking cakes, and I always lick the bowl!

Flourless Almond and Blueberry Cake

Flourless cakes typically have creamed egg yolks and sugar, with ground nuts and flavouring added. They are then lightened with whisked egg whites before baking. This is a simple but classic version.

PREP TIME: *30 minutes*
COOKING TIME: *50–60 minutes*
MAKES: *8–10 slices*

165G (¾ CUP) CASTER SUGAR

6 EGGS, SEPARATED

1 TSP FINELY GRATED LEMON ZEST

½ TSP ALMOND ESSENCE

½ TSP VANILLA EXTRACT

125G BUTTER, MELTED AND COOLED

250G (2 CUPS) ALMOND MEAL

PINCH OF SALT

75G (½ CUP) BLUEBERRIES (FRESH OR FROZEN)

ICING SUGAR, TO DUST

FRESH BLUEBERRIES AND THICK SWEETENED YOGURT, TO SERVE

1 Preheat oven to 170°C. Grease a 20cm (base measurement) round springform tin and line the base with baking paper.

2 Set aside 1 tablespoon of sugar to use with the egg whites. In the bowl of an electric mixer, combine the egg yolks and remaining sugar. Beat on high until the mixture is thick and creamy. Reduce the beater speed to low, and mix in the zest, almond essence and vanilla extract. Pour in the melted butter, followed by the almond meal, and fold through until well combined.

3 In a separate bowl, whisk the egg whites with a pinch of salt and the reserved tablespoon of sugar, until they form soft peaks. Stir a large spoonful through the almond mixture to 'loosen' it, then gently fold in the remaining egg whites.

4 Pour into the prepared cake tin and sprinkle with the blueberries (they should sink into the batter). Bake for 50–60 minutes, or until a skewer inserted in the centre comes out clean. If it appears to be browning too quickly, cover it loosely with foil for the remainder of the cooking time.

5 Cool in the tin for 10 minutes before releasing the sides and sliding onto a wire rack to cool completely. Dust with icing sugar and serve with fresh blueberries, and thick sweetened yogurt on the side.

NOTE

This cake is best prepared and eaten on the same day. I personally think it's best warm out of the oven! Using pure icing sugar keeps this recipe gluten-free.

Madeira Loaf Cake

The basics of cake baking are no better displayed than in the humble Madeira cake. Sadly, most people visualise the plastic-wrapped, highly processed version from supermarkets. This recipe, on the other hand, delivers the rustic charm of a country cake straight from the oven ... complete with wonderful aroma!

PREP TIME: *20 minutes*
COOKING TIME: *1 hour*
MAKES: *10–12 slices*

250G BUTTER, AT ROOM
TEMPERATURE, CHOPPED

220G (1 CUP) CASTER SUGAR

3 EGGS

225G (1½ CUPS)
SELF-RAISING FLOUR

100G (⅔ CUP) PLAIN FLOUR

1½ TBS LEMON JUICE

60ML (¼ CUP) MILK

1 TBS CASTER SUGAR,
FOR SPRINKLING

1 Preheat the oven to 170°C. Grease a 21cm x 10cm (base measurement) loaf tin and line the base with baking paper, extending over the two long sides.

2 In the bowl of an electric mixer, cream the butter and sugar until pale, scraping down the bowl as necessary. Add the eggs one at a time, beating well after each addition (it may look a bit curdled but the flour will bring it back to a good consistency).

3 Add the sifted flours and fold in until just incorporated. Add the lemon juice and fold through, then the milk.

4 Spoon into the prepared tin and sprinkle with the extra caster sugar. Bake for 1 hour, or until a skewer inserted in the centre comes out clean. Cool in the tin for 10 minutes before turning out onto a wire rack to cool completely.

NOTE

This cake is best eaten straight out of the oven, but does last 2–3 days in an airtight container. Try stirring through ½ punnet of fresh blueberries just before you spoon the mixture into the tin, or replace the lemon juice with orange juice and stir through the finely grated zest of an orange and a handful of slivered almonds. For the more adventurous, you could stir through 2 teaspoons of caraway seeds for something a bit different. The options are limited only by your imagination!

Bung-In Chocolate Cake

The first cake every child in my long family line learns to bake is affectionately known as 'The Bung-In Cake', which is a basic melt-and-mix cake. In my nanna's words, 'You just "bung" it all in together and it's done.' One of my children, at the age of two, could tell you what went into the bung-in cake ... that's how popular it is in my family!

PREP TIME: *30 minutes*
COOKING TIME: *40–50 minutes*
MAKES: *8–10 slices*

CAKE

300G (2 CUPS) SELF-RAISING FLOUR

330G (1½ CUPS) CASTER SUGAR

35G (⅓ CUP) COCOA POWDER

2 EGGS, LIGHTLY BEATEN

2 TSP VANILLA EXTRACT

330ML (1⅓ CUPS) MILK

150G BUTTER, MELTED

ICING

200G (1¼ CUPS) ICING SUGAR MIXTURE

2 TBS COCOA POWDER

30G BUTTER, MELTED

1 TSP VANILLA EXTRACT

2 TBS MILK

1 Preheat the oven to 180°C. Grease a 23cm (base measurement) square tin and line the base with baking paper.

2 Sift the dry ingredients into a bowl, and stir to combine. Make a well in the centre and add the wet ingredients. Whisk gently, gradually taking in the dry ingredients from the side of the bowl. Keep whisking until the mixture is smooth.

3 Pour the mixture into the prepared tin and bake for 40–50 minutes, or until a skewer inserted into the centre comes out clean. Cool in the tin for 10 minutes and then run a knife around the edge to separate the cake from the tin. Turn out onto a wire rack to cool completely.

4 To make the icing, sift the icing sugar and cocoa powder into a bowl. Add the melted butter and vanilla extract, and enough milk to get it to a paste consistency, stirring vigorously until smooth. You may not need all the milk. If it is too thick, add more milk. If it is too runny, add more icing mixture.

5 Once the cake has cooled, smother the top with chocolate icing.

NOTE

While it's always best warm out of the oven, it will keep well for 3-4 days. I often make two of these cakes at once, and freeze the spare one. My nanna often replaced some of the milk in the icing with a squeeze of lemon juice for a bit of 'zing'! You could also add orange zest to the cake, and replace the milk in the icing with orange juice for a jaffa cake.

Chocolate Self-Saucing Pudding

Traditional puddings are basically saucy cakes that are often steamed rather than baked. This can be done on a stove, or in the oven. This chocolate pudding is one of my ultimate comfort foods.

PREP TIME: *20 minutes*
COOKING TIME: *25 minutes*
MAKES: *4 serves*

1 TBS BROWN SUGAR

1 TBS COCOA POWDER

PUDDING BATTER

100G GOOD-QUALITY DARK CHOCOLATE, CHOPPED

50G BUTTER, CHOPPED

125ML (½ CUP) MILK

2 TBS COCOA POWDER

100G (⅔ CUP) SELF-RAISING FLOUR

75G (⅓ CUP) CASTER SUGAR

1 EGG, LIGHTLY BEATEN

TOPPING

55G (¼ CUP) BROWN SUGAR

35G (⅓ CUP) COCOA POWDER

180M (¾ CUP) BOILING WATER, PLUS EXTRA FOR CREATING A WATER BATH

GOOD-QUALITY VANILLA ICE CREAM, TO SERVE

1 Preheat the oven to 170°C. Combine 1 tablespoon of brown sugar and 1 tablespoon of cocoa powder in a bowl and stir to combine. Grease four 1-cup capacity ovenproof ramekins. Dust each ramekin with the cocoa and sugar mixture. Tip out any excess and discard.

2 For the pudding batter, combine the chocolate, butter, milk and cocoa powder in a medium saucepan. Stir gently over medium-low heat, until the chocolate and butter have melted and the mixture is smooth. Sift the flour and sugar into a medium-sized bowl. Add the egg and the chocolate mixture to the bowl and stir until smooth. Spoon evenly into the prepared ramekins and place into a large, deep baking dish.

3 For the topping, combine the ingredients in a jug and pour gently over the batter, ensuring a fairly equal amount goes onto each pudding. Pour extra boiling water into the baking dish around the ramekins, so that the water comes about halfway up the sides.

4 Carefully place into the oven and bake for 25 minutes, or until the top half is set and cooked through (remember the bottom should be saucy!).

5 Remove the ramekins from the baking dish, and allow them to cool for a minute. Serve with vanilla ice cream so it melts and oozes into the whole thing.

NOTE

The pudding batter can be made before guests arrive, but the topping and baking of the pudding should be done just before serving. A good tip is to place each ramekin onto a serving plate with a napkin under the ramekin to stop it slipping. It's very easy to add other subtle flavours to this pudding. Try substituting ¼ cup of the flour with hazelnut meal, and 50g of the chocolate with Nutella.

Beyond the basics...

Retro Coffee Cakes

These cakes hold a special place in my heart. Not only do they represent the day I fell in love with baking at the ripe old age of eight, but they also kick-started my MasterChef journey as they were the first dish I cooked in the MasterChef kitchen.

PREP TIME: *50 minutes*
COOKING TIME: *40 minutes*
MAKES: *9*

CAKE

250G BUTTER, AT ROOM TEMPERATURE, CHOPPED

220G (1 CUP) CASTER SUGAR

1 TSP VANILLA EXTRACT

2 EGGS

300G (2 CUPS) SELF-RAISING FLOUR

180ML (¾ CUP) ESPRESSO COFFEE, COOLED

COFFEE BUTTER CREAM

180G BUTTER, AT ROOM TEMPERATURE, CHOPPED

240G (1½ CUPS) ICING SUGAR MIXTURE, SIFTED

40ML (2 TBS) ESPRESSO COFFEE

1 TBS KAHLUA

40G (½ CUP) FLAKED ALMONDS, TOASTED

1 Preheat the oven to 170°C. Grease a 22cm (base measurement) square cake tin and line the base with baking paper.

2 To make the cake batter, cream the butter in an electric mixer on high speed until pale in colour (2–3 minutes). Reduce to medium speed and gradually add in the sugar and vanilla. Scrape the bowl down and then take the speed back up to high and beat again for 2–3 minutes until the sugar has dissolved into the butter. Add the eggs one at a time, beating well after each addition. Add the sifted flour, and mix on low speed until almost combined. Add the coffee gradually until the mixture has absorbed it all. Increase the speed and beat on high for 30 seconds.

3 Pour the mixture into the prepared tin and bake for 40 minutes or until a skewer inserted into the centre of the cake comes out clean. Cool in the tin for 5–10 minutes and then turn out onto a wire rack to cool completely.

4 To make the coffee butter cream, beat the butter with an electric mixer until pale and very light and creamy in texture. This will take 3–5 minutes on the highest speed. Add the sifted icing mixture and beat again until incorporated thoroughly. Reduce the speed to low and gradually add the coffee and Kahlua. It may initially curdle but don't worry! Increase the speed of your mixer back up to high and mix for another 2–3 minutes.

5 To assemble the cake, cut 9 circles out of the cake using a 9cm round cookie cutter. Slice each circle horizontally into 3 pieces and layer each with coffee butter cream. (If the butter cream has become a bit too stiff to spread, simply add a teaspoon or two of milk to loosen it up again.) Top with butter cream and sprinkle with toasted flaked almonds.

NOTE

These cakes are best eaten on the same day, but they will keep in an airtight container for 3 days or in the freezer for up to 3 months. For ease of serving, this could also be one large cake with frosting!

ear, Maple and Macadamia Upside-Down Cake

Upside-down cakes are such an efficient and delicious way to bake – when the cake is turned out, there's no need for any icing, as the topping is already built in!

PREP TIME: *40 minutes*
COOKING TIME: *about 1 hour*
MAKES: *10–12 slices*

TOPPING

110G (½ CUP) CASTER SUGAR

125ML (½ CUP) WATER

125ML (½ CUP) MAPLE SYRUP

75G BUTTER, CHOPPED

2 PEARS

40G (¼ CUP) MACADAMIAS, ROUGHLY CHOPPED

CAKE

3 EGGS

220G (1 CUP) CASTER SUGAR

1 TSP VANILLA EXTRACT

225G (1½ CUPS) SELF-RAISING FLOUR

125ML (½ CUP) MAPLE SYRUP

125G BUTTER, MELTED

2 RIPE PEARS, PEELED, CORED AND DICED

80G (½ CUP) MACADAMIAS, ROUGHLY CHOPPED

THICK DOUBLE CREAM, TO SERVE

1 Preheat the oven to 170°C. Grease a 23cm (base measurement) round cake tin (not springform, or the syrup will leak out) and line the base with baking paper.

2 To make the topping, combine the sugar and water in a small saucepan. Stir over low heat, without boiling, until the sugar has dissolved. Add the maple syrup and stir to combine. Increase the heat to medium and bring to the boil. Cook for 6–7 minutes, or until it is a rich golden brown colour. Take the saucepan off the heat and whisk in the butter. Keep whisking until it is all incorporated and slightly thickened.

3 To begin assembling the cake, pour about half the syrup mixture into the prepared cake tin, to a depth of about 5mm. Reserve the remaining syrup to serve. Peel and quarter the pears, removing the cores. Cut into 5mm-thick slices and arrange in a single layer in the syrup on the bottom of the tin (any excess pear can be chopped and stirred through the batter). Sprinkle the chopped macadamias over the pear.

4 To make the cake batter, beat the eggs, sugar and vanilla in the bowl of an electric mixer until thick and pale. Fold in the sifted flour, followed by the maple syrup, then the melted butter. Finally, stir through the pear pieces and macadamias.

5 Spoon the batter carefully over the pears and bake for about 1 hour, or until a skewer inserted into the centre comes out clean.

6 Allow the cake to stand in the tin for 5 minutes then turn out onto a serving plate. Drizzle with a little extra syrup and serve with a big dollop of thick double cream. You can serve any remaining syrup on the side.

NOTE

This cake is best served straight out of the oven, but it will keep for 2–3 days in an airtight container in the fridge. I advise warming gently before serving. For something different, try substituting the pears for apricot, peaches, banana or apple. And while you're at it, you could swap the macadamias for almonds, pecans or walnuts.

American Banana Bread with Walnuts

My husband, Luke, came home from work with a recipe for American Banana Bread from a fellow teacher who was visiting from the United States. She had made it for the staff morning tea, and we've been making my version of it ever since.

PREP TIME: *20 minutes*
COOKING TIME: *55 minutes*
MAKES: *8–10 slices*

100G BUTTER, AT ROOM TEMPERATURE, CHOPPED

220G (1 CUP) CASTER SUGAR

2 EGGS

2 VERY RIPE LARGE BANANAS, MASHED

1 TSP VANILLA EXTRACT

300G (2 CUPS) SELF-RAISING FLOUR

60ML (¼ CUP) BUTTERMILK (OR MILK WITH A SQUEEZE OF LEMON JUICE)

50G (½ CUP) WALNUTS, CHOPPED

1 Preheat the oven to 160°C. Grease a 21cm x 10cm (base measurement) loaf tin and line the base with baking paper, extending over the two long sides.

2 Use electric beaters to cream the butter and sugar until pale. Add the eggs one at a time, beating well after each addition. Mix in the mashed banana and vanilla extract. Sift the flour into the mixture. Add the buttermilk, and fold through until thoroughly combined. Stir through the walnuts.

3 Spoon into the loaf tin, and bake for 55 minutes, or until a skewer inserted in the centre comes out clean. Cool in the tin for 10 minutes, then turn out onto a wire rack to cool completely.

NOTE

This cake is best straight out of the oven, but on following days it's great toasted and slathered with butter! Feel free to try a different type of nut. Sometimes I use almonds or pecans. For a bit more decadence you can stir chopped dark chocolate through the batter before it's cooked.

Little Lemon Syrup Cakes

I love syrup cakes, as they are guaranteed to be moist and they often have a double hit of flavour!

PREP TIME: *30 minutes*
COOKING TIME: *20–25 minutes*
MAKES: *8*

CAKES

125G BUTTER, AT ROOM TEMPERATURE, CHOPPED

165G (¾ CUP) CASTER SUGAR

FINELY GRATED ZEST OF 1 LEMON

2 EGGS

185G (1¼ CUPS) SELF-RAISING FLOUR

PINCH OF SALT

80 ML (⅓ CUP) FRESH LEMON JUICE

SYRUP

80 ML (⅓ CUP) FRESH LEMON JUICE

1 TSP LEMON ZEST, OPTIONAL

110G (½ CUP) CASTER SUGAR

1 Preheat the oven to 170°C. Grease and flour 8 holes of large (½-cup capacity) muffin tins and line the bases with a small round of baking paper. (Alternatively, you can line the tin with paper muffin cases.)

2 Use electric beaters to cream together the butter, sugar and zest until pale. Add the eggs one at a time, beating well after each addition. Fold in the flour and salt, followed by the lemon juice.

3 Divide evenly among the muffin tins. Bake for 20–25 minutes, or until a skewer inserted in the centre of a cake comes out clean.

4 Meanwhile, to make the syrup, combine the lemon juice, zest and sugar in a small saucepan. Stir over low heat without boiling until the sugar has dissolved. Increase the heat to medium and simmer for 1 minute.

5 As soon as the cakes come out of the oven, loosen them from the edge of the tin. Prick them with a skewer all over and then spoon the syrup evenly over each cake (you may not use up all the syrup).

6 Allow the cakes to cool for 5–10 minutes in the tin, then transfer to a wire rack, discarding the small round of baking paper.

NOTE

These are better made a little ahead of time. They are best eaten on the same day they are made, but are still pretty good 2–3 days later. Other zesty flavours like orange and lime work well. Just substitute the zest and juice accordingly. One medium lemon should yield about 80ml (⅓ cup) juice.

White Chocolate and Almond Dessert Cake

This flourless cake is rich and dense so it makes the perfect dessert cake. I like to serve it simply with some thick double cream and fresh berries.

PREP TIME: *25 minutes*
COOKING TIME: *50 minutes*
MAKES: *8 slices*

165G (¾ CUP) CASTER SUGAR

200G GOOD-QUALITY WHITE CHOCOLATE, CHOPPED

150G BUTTER, CHOPPED

5 EGGS, SEPARATED

1 TSP FINELY GRATED ORANGE ZEST

90G (¾ CUP) ALMOND MEAL

ICING SUGAR, TO DUST

THICK DOUBLE CREAM AND FRESH BERRIES, TO SERVE

1 Preheat the oven to 170°C. Grease a 22cm (base measurement) square tin and line the base and sides with baking paper.

2 Set aside 1 tablespoon of sugar and then combine the remaining sugar, chocolate and butter in a heatproof bowl and place over a saucepan of gently simmering water (don't let the base of the bowl touch the water). Stir occasionally until it is all melted and smooth. Remove from the heat and cool slightly. Whisk in the egg yolks, one at a time, mixing well after each addition. Add the orange zest and almond meal and stir thoroughly.

3 In a separate bowl, beat the egg whites with the reserved 1 tablespoon of sugar until soft peaks form. Stir a large spoonful of egg white into the chocolate mixture to 'loosen' it and then gently fold in the remaining egg white.

4 Pour into the prepared tin and bake for 50 minutes, or until a skewer inserted into the centre comes out clean. If it's browning too quickly, simply cover it loosely with foil while it continues to cook.

5 Cool the cake in the tin and then invert briefly onto a chopping board, then invert again so it is right-side up on another board. Cut in half and then into triangular pieces and serve dusted with icing sugar, with thickened double cream and fresh berries.

NOTE

For something a little bit different, try serving this with passionfruit curd (see page 64). Using pure icing sugar keeps this recipe gluten-free.

Brown Butter Cheesecake

A cookbook full of sweet recipes would not be complete without a cheesecake. While technically not really a 'cake', it does have the word in its name so I'm taking that as qualification! The brown butter adds a slightly savoury element to this baked cheesecake, which I love, as I think some cheesecakes are just too sweet. It's supposed to be a rustic cheesecake so don't be too worried about cracks and bumps – they all add to the character!

PREP TIME: *25 minutes*

COOKING TIME: *1 hour 15 minutes + cooling*

REFRIGERATING TIME: *3 hours minimum (preferably overnight)*

MAKES: *8 pieces*

300G BUTTER, CHOPPED

BISCUIT BASE

250G SCOTCH FINGER BISCUITS

FILLING

500G CREAM CHEESE, AT ROOM TEMPERATURE, CHOPPED

4 EGGS, SEPARATED

2 TSP VANILLA EXTRACT

2 TBS CASTER SUGAR

1½ TBS CORNFLOUR

120G (½ CUP) SOUR CREAM

PINCH OF SALT

1   Preheat the oven to 150°C. Lightly spray a 20cm (base measurement) springform tin and line the base with baking paper.

2   To make the brown butter, place the butter into a medium saucepan over medium heat. First the butter will melt, then it will bubble quite loudly, and then it will go quiet and foam on the top. You need to stir it at intervals from this point to stop the milk solids from sticking to the bottom of the pan. Underneath the foam it will become a nut-brown colour. (It takes 1–2 minutes from when it has foamed.) Take it off the heat and pour into a heat-proof measuring jug, and within a couple of minutes the foam will subside.

3   For the biscuit base, roughly break the Scotch Finger biscuits into the bowl of a food processor and process to fine crumbs. With the motor running, pour 125ml (½ cup) of the brown butter into the food processor and process until crumbs are evenly moistened. Press into the base of the prepared tin and refrigerate until needed.

4   For the filling, place the cream cheese, egg yolks, vanilla, caster sugar and cornflour into the bowl of an electric mixer, and beat until smooth. Add the remaining cooled brown butter and the sour cream, and mix until just combined.

5   In a separate bowl, whisk the egg whites and salt to firm peaks. Fold the egg whites into the cream cheese mixture until just combined.

6   Pour the mixture onto the biscuit base and bake for 1 hour 15 minutes, until golden on top. Turn off the oven and let the cheesecake cool in the oven for 2 hours. Remove from the oven and cool to room temperature, then refrigerate for about 3 hours (or overnight), until chilled.

NOTE

This can be made ahead of time and kept in the fridge for up to 3 days.

Nanna's Christmas Pudding

A dessert cookbook from me wouldn't be complete without Nanna's Christmas Pudding. This was the dessert that convinced me that fruit in a cake was a good thing! It may have had something to do with the old coins hidden inside that Nanna swapped for 'real' money, but even now, as an adult, I love this pudding, coins or not. It does have a long cooking time (8 hours), but I think it's worth the effort.

PREP TIME: *1 hour + overnight soaking*
COOKING TIME: *8 hours*
MAKES: *10–12 slices*

THE FRUIT

250G RAISINS

250G CURRANTS

250G SULTANAS

60ML (¼ CUP) RUM

THE MIXTURE

250G BUTTER, AT ROOM TEMPERATURE, CHOPPED

250G (1 CUP FIRMLY PACKED + 1 TBS) BROWN SUGAR

4 EGGS

125G (1¾ CUPS) FRESH WHITE BREADCRUMBS

125G PLAIN FLOUR, SIFTED

PINCH OF SALT

1 TSP NUTMEG

2 TSP MIXED SPICE

1 TSP FINELY GRATED LEMON ZEST

PREPARING THE FRUIT (THE DAY BEFORE)

1 Cut the raisins in half and place into a bowl with the currants and sultanas. Cover with rum and leave to soak overnight.

LINING THE BASIN

2 Grease a 2-litre capacity (8 cup) pudding basin with butter and dust with flour. I use an old one belonging to Nanna but you can buy them now with tight-fitting lids, which are much easier to use. Line the base with 2 layers of baking paper cut to fit neatly.

MAKING THE MIXTURE

3 Use electric beaters to cream the butter and sugar until pale. Add the eggs one at a time, beating well after each addition.

4 Stir in the soaked fruit mixture and then fold in the dry ingredients and lemon zest. Pour into the prepared basin, adding washed coins as you go (see note). Level the surface of the pudding.

SEALING THE BASIN

5 If your pudding basin has a lid, grease it and place securely on top. Otherwise, cut 2 pieces of greaseproof paper at least 5cm larger than the top of the basin, and grease well (or you can use baking paper). Make a pleat across the centre. Place over the top of the basin and tie tightly around with string. Tear a large piece of foil, pleat it across the centre and place over the greaseproof paper. Tie with string and make a handle of string across the top of the basin.

COOKING THE PUDDING

6 Place a trivet (or something to keep the base of the pudding off the base of the saucepan – I use a shallow upside-down heatproof bowl) into the base of a large saucepan that will fit the pudding basin in it with plenty of room for water.

7 Place the pudding basin onto the trivet in the pan. Pour enough boiling water into the pan to come roughly halfway up the side of the pudding basin.

→

8 Cover the pan with a lid and bring to a gentle simmer. Cook for 8 hours, checking water levels every hour, and top up with boiling water so that it remains at the same level and continues to simmer gently.

9 At the end of the 8 hours, remove the pudding from the saucepan (taking care not to burn yourself!) and leave it to cool to room temperature. Store in the pudding basin, wrapped so that it is airtight, in the refrigerator for up to 3 months for the flavours to develop.

SERVING

10 Invert the pudding onto a plate and microwave for 10 minutes to heat it. Immediately prior to serving, drizzle with a little rum and light with a match to make it flame. Serve with brandy custard, whipped cream and vanilla ice cream. (Yes, you need all three!)

NOTE

This is best made well ahead of time to allow the flavours to develop. Nanna used to make it in September, ready for Christmas Day. It should be kept airtight in the fridge. I've kept the layout in Nanna's original form too because it works – she was ordered in everything she did. Contemporary coins cannot be used in the pudding because of the toxins, so they must be the old, original pennies and sixpences. You can buy food-safe pudding 'coins' from some specialty food or kitchenware shops.

Raspberry and White Chocolate Puddings

Raspberries would have to be my all-time favourite fruit, so I use them whenever I have the opportunity. These decadent little puddings are such great comfort food, in my opinion.

PREP TIME: *30 minutes*
COOKING TIME: *25–30 minutes*
MAKES: *6*

RASPBERRY SAUCE

110G (½ CUP) CASTER SUGAR

125ML (½ CUP) WATER

125G RASPBERRIES,
PLUS 18 RASPBERRIES,
PLUS EXTRA TO SERVE

1 TSP LEMON JUICE

PUDDINGS

110G (½ CUP) CASTER SUGAR

125G BUTTER, AT ROOM
TEMPERATURE, CHOPPED

1 TSP VANILLA EXTRACT

2 EGGS, SEPARATED

75G (½ CUP)
SELF-RAISING FLOUR

125ML (½ CUP) MILK

100G WHITE CHOCOLATE,
GRATED

1   For the raspberry sauce, combine the sugar and water in a small saucepan and stir over medium-low heat, without boiling, until the sugar has dissolved. Increase the heat to a simmer and cook a further minute.

2   Remove the saucepan from the heat and add about half the raspberries (60g). Crush gently with a wooden spoon and then set aside for the mixture to cool to room temperature.

3   Strain the raspberry liquid through a sieve, discarding the solids. Add the remaining raspberries (60g) and the lemon juice to the cooled raspberry liquid and process until smooth.

4   Preheat the oven to 170°C and grease 6 holes in a Texas muffin tin (⅔–¾ cup capacity).

5   For the pudding batter, set aside 1 tablespoon of sugar for beating with the egg whites. In the bowl of an electric mixer, cream the butter on high speed for 2–3 minutes, until pale. Lower the speed to medium and gradually add the remaining sugar and the vanilla extract. Increase the speed to high again and beat for a further 1 minute, scraping down the sides of the bowl as necessary. Add the egg yolks and beat again until they are well combined and the mixture is smooth. Add the flour, milk and grated white chocolate and mix on low speed until just smooth.

6   In a separate bowl, beat the egg whites and the reserved 1 tablespoon of sugar to firm peaks. Fold a large spoonful into the cake mixture to 'loosen' it, and then fold in the remaining egg white until fully incorporated.

7   To assemble the puddings, spoon 1 tablespoon of raspberry sauce into the base of each muffin tin. Place the remaining sauce into a small saucepan and cook over low-medium heat for 5 minutes until syrupy. Divide half the batter between the muffin tins. Top with 3 raspberries, then add the remaining batter. Stand the muffin tin in a large baking dish and pour boiling water into the dish so that it comes halfway up the sides of the muffin tin. Bake for 25–30 minutes, until the top of each pudding springs back when touched lightly. Carefully remove the muffin tin from the baking dish and cool for 5 minutes.

→

8 Run a knife around the edge of each pudding to loosen, then invert carefully onto a chopping board. Note that they can look a little strange with the syrup soaked into the cake, but it all gets hidden when you top it with extra syrup! Transfer each pudding to a serving plate and top with an extra spoonful of raspberry syrup. Serve with extra raspberries.

NOTE

These puddings are best eaten straight out of the oven, but will keep for up to 3 days refrigerated in an airtight container. Warm them slightly before serving, if storing beforehand.

Sare's Melting Moments

Choc-Chunk Cookies

Cranberry, White Chocolate
and Macadamia Cookies

Salted Caramel, Almond and
Chocolate Slice

Chocolate Macadamia Brownies

Hazelnut Cream Biscuits

Flat-Pack Gingerbread Houses

Jaffa Muffins

Amaretti

Vanilla Cupcakes with
Vanilla Cream Butter

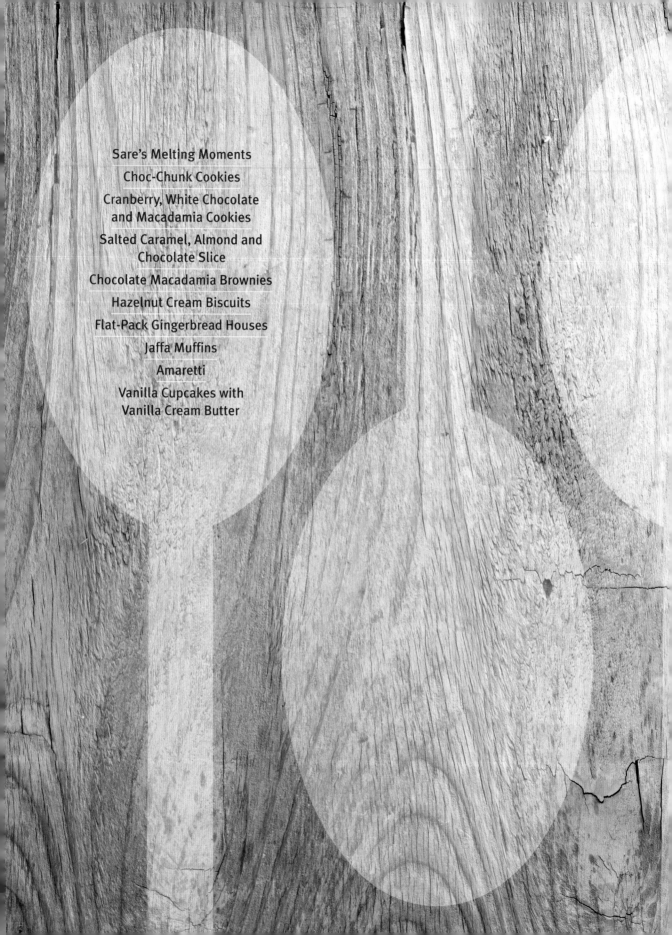

Baked treats

There's something
very welcoming about walking
into a kitchen with the oven roaring
and the sight and aroma of freshly
baked goods sitting on the kitchen
bench. With years of baking
heritage behind many of us, it's
virtually impossible to summarise
the techniques involved as they are
so many and so varied.

So this chapter is simply a
collection of some of my favourite
baked treats. I hope you enjoy
baking them as
much as I do.

Sare's Melting Moments

Years ago Luke's sister Sare made the most memorable melting moments I'd ever eaten. I asked for the recipe and I've been making versions of them ever since.

PREP TIME: *20 minutes*
COOKING TIME: *20 minutes*
 + 1 hour setting
MAKES: *12*

250G COLD BUTTER, CHOPPED

55G (⅓ CUP) ICING SUGAR
MIXTURE

1 TSP VANILLA EXTRACT

260G (1¾ CUPS) PLAIN FLOUR

40G (⅓ CUP) CUSTARD POWDER

FILLING

60G BUTTER, AT ROOM
TEMPERATURE, CHOPPED

½ TSP VANILLA EXTRACT

FINELY GRATED ZEST OF 1 LEMON

110G (⅔ CUP) ICING SUGAR
MIXTURE, PLUS EXTRA TO DUST.

1 Preheat the oven to 160°C. Grease 2 large baking trays and line with baking paper.

2 Place the butter, icing sugar and vanilla into the bowl of an electric mixer and beat until combined. Don't overbeat or the mixture will become too soft. Sift in the flour and custard powder and mix until just combined and it holds together when you pinch a small amount in your fingers.

3 Roll level tablespoons of mixture into balls and place onto the trays, leaving space between them as they will spread a little. You should have 24. Press each one lightly on the top with the back of a fork, dusting the fork with icing sugar to prevent it from sticking to the dough.

4 Bake for 20 minutes, until just starting to turn golden and cooked right through. (I normally sacrifice one, cutting it in half so that I can be sure it's cooked, and it usually involves a taste test too!)

5 Leave them on the tray for 10 minutes, and then carefully transfer to a wire rack to cool completely.

6 To make the filling, combine the butter, vanilla and zest in the bowl of an electric mixer and mix until pale and creamy. Add the icing sugar and beat on high for 1 minute until thoroughly incorporated.

7 Sandwich two cooled biscuits together with 2 teaspoons of the filling. Repeat with the remaining biscuits. Dust all of them lightly with icing sugar. Store the biscuits in an airtight container in the fridge to set for a minimum of 1 hour.

NOTE

These can be made ahead of time and stored in an airtight container in the fridge for up to 2 weeks. Orange or lime zest could be substituted for the lemon zest for a slightly different flavour, as could vanilla or strawberry essence.

Choc-Chunk Cookies (Liam's favourite)

Choc-chip cookies (pictured on previous page) have always been a weakness of mine. Years ago, as I was making a batch, I found that I didn't have any choc-chips in the cupboard – but I did have a block of chocolate. I proceeded to chop the chocolate into chunks and have never used choc-chips since.

PREP TIME: *20 minutes*
COOKING TIME: *12–15 minutes*
MAKES: *about 30*

125G BUTTER, AT ROOM
TEMPERATURE, CHOPPED

110G (½ CUP) CASTER SUGAR

110G (½ CUP) BROWN SUGAR

1 TSP VANILLA EXTRACT

1 EGG

260G (1¾ CUPS)
SELF-RAISING FLOUR

180G DARK CHOCOLATE

1   Preheat the oven to 175°C. Grease 2 large baking trays and line with baking paper.

2   Combine the butter, both sugars and the vanilla in the bowl of an electric mixer and beat until pale. Add the egg and beat until well combined, scraping down the bowl as necessary. Sift the flour into the bowl and mix until just combined.

3   Cut the chocolate into 1cm-wide lengths diagonally across the block. It will naturally shatter a little. Then cut in the same way in the opposite direction. This way you get random-sized 'chunks' of chocolate. Tip the whole lot in and mix through.

4   Gather the dough together and roll level tablespoons of mixture into balls. Place onto the prepared trays, leaving space between them for spreading.

5   Bake for 12–15 minutes until golden (12 minutes will make them slightly softer, 15 minutes will give you crispier cookies). Leave on the trays for 5 minutes, then transfer to a wire rack to cool completely.

NOTE

These can be stored in an airtight container for up to 1 week. The dough (before it is cooked) can be rolled into balls and frozen for up to 3 months. You could easily substitute white chocolate or milk chocolate if you prefer.

Cranberry, White Chocolate and Macadamia Cookies

These little cookies (pictured on following page) are great any time of the year, but for some reason I especially like them at Christmas. There's something about the red and white that makes them look very festive!

PREP TIME: *20 minutes*
COOKING TIME: *12–15 minutes*
MAKES: *about 30*

125G BUTTER, AT ROOM TEMPERATURE, CHOPPED

165G (¾ CUP) CASTER SUGAR

½ TSP VANILLA EXTRACT

½ TSP FINELY GRATED ORANGE ZEST

1 EGG

260G (1¾ CUPS) SELF-RAISING FLOUR

80G WHITE CHOCOLATE, CHOPPED INTO CHUNKS

50G MACADAMIAS, ROUGHLY CHOPPED

50G DRIED CRANBERRIES (CRAISINS)

1 Preheat the oven to 175°C. Grease 2 large baking trays and line with baking paper.

2 Combine the butter, sugar, vanilla and orange zest in the bowl of an electric mixer and beat until pale. Add the egg and beat until well combined, scraping down the bowl as necessary. Sift the flour into the bowl and mix until just combined.

3 Add the chocolate, macadamias and cranberries to the mixture and mix it through.

4 Gather the dough together and roll level tablespoons of mixture into balls. Place onto the prepared trays, allowing space for spreading.

5 Bake for 12–15 minutes until golden (12 minutes will make them slightly softer, 15 minutes will give you crispier cookies). Leave on the trays for 5 minutes before transferring to a wire rack to cool completely.

NOTE

These can be stored in an airtight container for up to 1 week. The dough (before it is cooked) can be rolled into balls and frozen for up to 3 months.

Salted Caramel, Almond and Chocolate Slice

I do love my retro sweets, so I've taken another one and added my own little twist.

PREP TIME: *40 minutes*
COOKING TIME: *35 minutes + 2 hours setting*
MAKES: *32 small square pieces*

BASE

75G (½ CUP) SELF-RAISING FLOUR

60G (½ CUP) ALMOND MEAL

110G (½ CUP) BROWN SUGAR

60G BUTTER, MELTED

FILLING

2 X 395G CANS CONDENSED MILK

60G BUTTER

80ML (⅓ CUP) GOLDEN SYRUP

1 ½ TSP SEA SALT FLAKES

50G SLIVERED ALMONDS, TOASTED

TOPPING

125G DARK CHOCOLATE, CHOPPED

30G BUTTER, CHOPPED

½ TSP SEA SALT FLAKES, TO SPRINKLE

1 TBS FLAKED ALMONDS, TOASTED, TO SPRINKLE

1 Preheat the oven to 175°C. Grease a 26cm x 16cm (base measurement) slice tin, and line the base with baking paper, extending over the two long sides.

2 For the base, place the flour, almond meal and brown sugar into a food processor and process briefly to combine. With the motor running, pour in the melted butter, processing until evenly moistened. Tip the mixture into the prepared tin and press down firmly with the back of a spoon. Bake for 15 minutes then set aside to cool while you make the filling.

3 To make the filling, combine the condensed milk, butter and golden syrup in a medium saucepan and stir over medium-low heat until melted and combined. Increase the heat so that the mixture bubbles occasionally, and stir constantly with a soft spatula for about 8 minutes, until the mixture thickens and starts to change colour. I find that if I walk away from it, it inevitably sticks on the bottom of the pan, and I end up with burnt bits and having to start again!

4 Stir in the salt and the almonds and then pour the mixture over the cooled base. Return it to the oven for 10 minutes. Set aside to cool for 5 minutes.

5 To make the topping, combine the chocolate and butter in a microwave-safe bowl. Cook on high for 30 seconds and then stir. Continue to cook in 30-second bursts, stirring in between, until the chocolate and butter have melted and the mixture is smooth. Pour onto the filling and smooth out. Sprinkle with extra salt and slivered almonds. Cool to room temperature, then refrigerate for about 2 hours, until set. Cut into small squares to serve.

NOTE

This can be made ahead of time and kept in an airtight container for up to 1 week.

Chocolate Macadamia Brownies

I have loved chocolate for as long as I can remember. One of my favourite ways to eat chocolate is as a brownie. Its fudgy texture with hits of chewiness and soft crunch are virtually unbeatable in my book.

PREP TIME: *20 minutes*
COOKING TIME: *45 minutes*
MAKES: *12 pieces*

125G BUTTER, CHOPPED

125G DARK CHOCOLATE, CHOPPED

220G (1 CUP) CASTER SUGAR

3 EGGS, SEPARATED

½ TSP VANILLA EXTRACT

50G (⅓ CUP) PLAIN FLOUR

2 TBS SELF-RAISING FLOUR

25G (¼ CUP) DARK COCOA POWDER (SEE NOTE)

70G (½ CUP) MACADAMIAS, ROUGHLY CHOPPED

80G WHITE CHOCOLATE, ROUGHLY CHOPPED

PINCH OF SALT

2 TSP DARK COCOA POWDER, TO DUST (SEE NOTE)

1 Preheat the oven to 160°C. Grease a 20cm square cake tin and line the base and sides with baking paper.

2 Place the butter and chocolate in a microwave-safe bowl. Microwave for 30 seconds and then stir. Continue to cook in 30-second bursts, stirring in between, until melted and smooth. Cool slightly.

3 Reserve 1 tablespoon of sugar to whisk with the egg whites. Add the remaining sugar, egg yolks and vanilla to the chocolate mixture and whisk to combine thoroughly.

4 Sift the flours and cocoa powder over the top, and fold in until well combined. Fold in the macadamias and white chocolate.

5 In a separate bowl, whisk the egg whites, salt and reserved tablespoon of sugar to soft peaks. Fold one third of the egg whites into the chocolate mixture to 'loosen' it, and then fold in the remaining two-thirds until just combined.

6 Spoon into the prepared tin and smooth the surface. Bake for 45 minutes, until the top has set and there is just the slightest wobble under its surface.

7 Cool in the tin for 15 minutes, then carefully lift out. Dust the top with dark cocoa powder, and cut into 12 rectangles.

NOTE

These can be made ahead of time and stored in an airtight container for up to 1 week. Dark cocoa powder is also known as Dutch or Dutch-processed cocoa. It has a rich, deep colour and flavour, and is available from delis and specialty food shops. Feel free to swap the nuts and white chocolate with other ingredients. Try fresh cherries and dark chocolate chunks, or walnuts and milk chocolate. For the purist, simply leave the additions out altogether! I also like to stir chopped-up pieces of brownie through softened ice cream before re-freezing it and serving it as a luscious dessert.

Hazelnut Cream Biscuits

A local café serve these gorgeous-tasting little biscuits, and when I tried my first one I was determined to come home and work out how to make them. So here is my version.

PREP TIME: *40 minutes*
COOKING TIME: *20 minutes*
MAKES: *about 14*

200G HAZELNUTS (SEE NOTE)

3 EGG WHITES

PINCH OF SALT

165G (¾ CUP) CASTER SUGAR

60G (½ CUP) ALMOND MEAL

250G BUTTER, AT ROOM
TEMPERATURE, CHOPPED

320G (2 CUPS) ICING SUGAR
MIXTURE, SIFTED

2½ TBS FRANGELICO

80G (½ CUP) ICING SUGAR,
FOR DUSTING

1 Preheat the oven to 160°C. Grease 2 large baking trays and line with baking paper.

2 To prepare the hazelnuts, place them into a dry frying pan and toast over medium-low heat for 5–10 minutes, stirring regularly, until they are lightly coloured and fragrant. Tip them into a clean tea towel and rub most of their skins off. Place the cooled hazelnuts into a food processor and process until finely ground. These hazelnuts will be used in 3 ways: 60g (½ cup) in the biscuits; 30g (¼ cup) in the hazelnut cream; and 110g (almost 1 cup) to roll the biscuits in at the end.

3 For the biscuit batter, place the egg whites and salt into the bowl of an electric mixer with a whisk attachment. Whisk on high speed for 2 minutes, until the egg whites form soft peaks. Reduce the speed to medium, and gradually add the sugar a spoonful at a time until it is all incorporated. Increase the speed to high again, and whisk for a further 4 minutes, until the meringue is thick and glossy. Fold in 60g (½ cup) of the ground hazelnuts and the almond meal.

4 Spoon level tablespoons of the mixture onto the prepared trays, spreading and smoothing to 4cm rounds. Leave a little space between each as they will spread slightly in the oven. You should have 28 rounds. Bake for 20 minutes, until the surface has set. Cool completely on the trays. They should be slightly moist inside.

5 Place the butter in an electric mixer and beat on high speed until pale and creamy. Add the icing sugar and beat again for a further 1 minute. Reduce the speed to low, and add 30g (¼ cup) of the ground hazelnuts and the Frangelico. Mix until combined.

6 Sandwich 2 biscuits together with hazelnut cream. Spread a little extra hazelnut cream around the edge of the sandwich and then roll the sides in the remaining ground hazelnuts. Repeat with remaining biscuits, filling and hazelnuts. Sit the biscuits flat on a plate or board and dust liberally with icing sugar before serving.

NOTE

These can be made ahead of time and kept in an airtight container for up to 1 week in the fridge. To save time and effort you can use ground hazelnuts.

Flat-Pack Gingerbread Houses

I did wonder if I would ever make a gingerbread house again, after Adriano Zumbo put me through my paces, but with young children in the house, I really had to face my fears! So I've come up with this version that brings all the joy of a gingerbread house while limiting all likely disasters. I've gone the more demure approach of decorating simply with white chocolate, but there's no reason you couldn't let some kids go to town covering them with lollies!

PREP TIME: *45 minutes*
RESTING TIME: *4 hours minimum
(preferably overnight)*
COOKING TIME: *10–15 minutes*
MAKES: *4 large houses or
6 small houses*

110G (½ CUP) CASTER SUGAR

60ML (¼ CUP) GOLDEN SYRUP

125ML (½ CUP) THICKENED
CREAM

1 TSP GROUND CINNAMON

¼ TSP GROUND CLOVES

1½ TSP GROUND GINGER

½ TSP BI-CARB SODA

60G BUTTER, CHOPPED

225G (1½ CUPS) PLAIN FLOUR

150G WHITE CHOCOLATE,
ROUGHLY CHOPPED

ASSORTED LOLLIES AND SWEETS,
TO DECORATE

1 Combine the sugar, golden syrup, cream and spices in a saucepan over low heat, stirring occasionally, until smooth. Bring to a simmer and cook gently for 3 minutes. Add the bi-carb and butter, and stir until the butter has melted.

2 Tip the mixture into an electric stand mixer and add the sifted flour. Beat on low speed for about 5 minutes, until it cools down slightly and becomes a thick paste consistency.

3 Meanwhile, prepare a tray at least 20cm x 20cm by lining it with a large sheet of plastic wrap, extending well over the sides. Scrape the mixture out of the bowl onto the plastic wrap, and wrap it up in a flat disc shape. Refrigerate for a minimum of 4 hours, or overnight, until firm enough to roll.

4 Once the gingerbread has chilled, preheat the oven to 180°C. Grease 2 large baking trays and line with baking paper.

5 In preparation for cutting the gingerbread into houses, make yourself a template out of paper. For a small house it should be 15cm high and 9cm wide. (Or you could make large houses 22cm high and 15cm wide.)

6 On a lightly floured surface, roll out half the dough to 3–4mm thickness. Use your template to cut into desired shapes. Lift onto the prepared trays. Repeat with the remaining dough. If you like, cut out windows and score 'brickwork' to give your house its own unique character.

7 Bake for 10–15 minutes, or until the surface is firm to the touch. Remove from the oven and cool completely.

8 When ready to decorate, melt the white chocolate by placing it in a microwave-safe bowl and microwaving on high in 30-second bursts, stirring in between, until the chocolate is melted and smooth.

9 Pour the chocolate into a small piping bag to decorate. (Alternatively, use the chocolate to stick lollies onto the gingerbread house in any design you like.) Leave it flat for at least 1 hour for the chocolate to set. Wrap as gifts or enjoy straight away!

Jaffa Muffins

Muffins are such a versatile sweet treat. You can make just about any flavour and they require only very basic kitchen equipment and a muffin tin.

PREP TIME: *25 minutes*
COOKING TIME: *20 minutes*
MAKES: *12*

300G (2 CUPS)
SELF-RAISING FLOUR

165G (¾ CUP) CASTER SUGAR

240G (1 CUP) SOUR CREAM

2 EGGS

80ML (⅓ CUP) VEGETABLE OIL

FINELY GRATED ZEST OF
1 ORANGE

100G DARK CHOCOLATE,
CHOPPED INTO CHUNKS

1 Preheat oven to 170°C, and line 12 holes of large (½-cup capacity) muffin tins with paper cases.

2 Sift the flour into a mixing bowl and stir in the sugar. Make a well in the centre.

3 Whisk the sour cream, eggs, vegetable oil and zest in a large jug until smooth. Pour this mixture and the chocolate chunks into the dry ingredients and mix with a large spoon until just combined.

4 Spoon the mixture into the muffin tins, dividing it evenly. Bake for 20 minutes, or until golden and springy to a gentle touch.

5 Cool in the tin for 5 minutes and then lift out onto a wire rack to cool completely.

NOTE

Muffins are best eaten the same day they are made, but will keep in an airtight container for up to 3 days.
Try different flavours by substituting the orange zest and chocolate for:
– finely grated zest of 1 lemon and 2 tablespoons of poppy seeds
– 125g fresh or frozen raspberries and 100g chopped white chocolate
– 1 cup of mashed overripe bananas and 60g (½ cup) chopped pecans.

Amaretti

Amaretti are Italian almond biscuits and they make such a versatile addition to any home cook's repertoire. They can be served simply by themselves as an accompaniment to a cup of coffee, or they can be served with a multitude of desserts to give extra flavour and texture. I like mine to be slightly chewy, but if you prefer them crisp just cook them a little longer.

PREP TIME: *20 minutes*
COOKING TIME: *20 minutes*
MAKES: *about 16*

280G (2 CUPS)
SLIVERED ALMONDS

55G (⅓ CUP)
ICING SUGAR MIXTURE

2 EGG WHITES

PINCH OF SALT

110G (½ CUP) CASTER SUGAR

1 TSP ALMOND ESSENCE

40G (½ CUP) FLAKED ALMONDS

EXTRA ICING SUGAR MIXTURE,
TO DUST

1 Preheat the oven to 160°C. Grease a large baking tray and line with baking paper.

2 Spread the slivered almonds onto the tray. Bake for about 10 minutes, stirring them occasionally, until golden and fragrant. Transfer to a plate to cool, then place into a food processor with the icing sugar. Process to fine crumbs.

3 Place the egg whites and salt into the bowl of an electric mixer with a whisk attachment and whisk on high speed until soft peaks form. Reduce the speed to medium and gradually add the caster sugar, one spoonful at a time, until it is all incorporated. Scrape down the bowl and then increase the speed to high again and beat for a further 4 minutes, until the mixture is thick and glossy.

4 Stir in the almond essence and the ground almond mixture until thoroughly combined. It will be almost the consistency of crunchy peanut butter.

5 Spoon level tablespoons of the mixture onto the prepared baking tray, and sprinkle liberally with flaked almonds. Bake for 20 minutes, until they are firm and can be peeled off the baking paper easily. Cool completely before dusting liberally with icing sugar.

Vanilla Cupcakes with Vanilla Cream Butter

Who doesn't love a good cupcake? They're ideal for birthdays, social events or for a special afternoon tea. I personally love the vanilla variety, but you can also use this as a base recipe to make just about any flavour you like.

PREP TIME: *30 minutes*
COOKING TIME: *18–20 minutes*
MAKES: *12*

CUPCAKES

125G BUTTER, AT ROOM TEMPERATURE, CHOPPED

150G (⅔ CUP) CASTER SUGAR

2 TSP VANILLA EXTRACT

3 EGGS

225G (1½ CUPS) SELF-RAISING FLOUR

60ML (¼ CUP) POURING CREAM

VANILLA BUTTER CREAM

180G BUTTER, AT ROOM TEMPERATURE, CHOPPED

240G (1½ CUPS) ICING SUGAR MIXTURE

2 TSP VANILLA EXTRACT

1 Preheat the oven to 175°C, and line 12 holes of medium (⅓-cup capacity) muffin tins with paper cases.

2 Place the butter and caster sugar into the bowl of an electric stand mixer and beat on high speed until pale and creamy, scraping down the sides of the bowl as necessary. Add vanilla and beat a further 1 minute on high speed. Reduce the speed to medium and add the eggs, one at a time, beating well after each addition. Add the flour and reduce the speed to low. With the beaters still running, pour in the cream. Beat on high for 30 seconds until smooth.

3 Spoon the batter into the patty cases. Bake for 18–20 minutes until golden and springy to a gentle touch. Lift out onto a wire rack to cool.

4 To make the vanilla butter cream, beat the butter until creamy, then add the icing sugar and vanilla, and beat until well combined. Spread the cooled cakes with the butter cream, making sure you get lots of swirls!

NOTE

These are best eaten the day they are made, but they will keep in an airtight container for up to 3 days. By adding a few drops of food colouring to the butter cream, and topping with your child's favourite lollies, these become a whole new treat.

Chocolate Terrine
with Spiced Praline,
Mandarin Oil and Crème Fraîche

Buttered Popcorn Ice Cream
with Bitter Caramel and
Salted Almond Crumb

Raspberry and Hazelnut Tarts
with Poached Meringue
and Frangelico Syrup

A sweet ending

For all those
like-minded wanna-be
chefs out there, this chapter is
for you! I've included just 3 recipes
that show you how you can put various
techniques together, explore new
flavour combinations and play around
with plating. What you end up with is
a dessert you might possibly see in a
restaurant (or B&B!). Alternatively, you
can choose one element and create your
own dessert around it. For me, there is a
lot of joy to be had from being creative —
and then sharing the results with
the people I love. We don't claim
to be chefs but we can
have fun trying!

Chocolate Terrine with Spiced Praline, Mandarin Oil and Crème Fraîche (my favourite)

The Mexicans have added spices to chocolate for a very long time, but it's something that hadn't really occurred to me until I tasted a wonderful example of it. This dessert takes that experience, makes it my own, and turns it into a recipe I will keep forever.

PREP TIME: *45 minutes*
COOKING TIME: *1 hour 15 minutes + cooling*
MAKES: *6 serves*

CHOCOLATE TERRINE

200G DARK COUVERTURE CHOCOLATE, ROUGHLY CHOPPED (SEE NOTE)

130G BUTTER, CHOPPED

4 EGG YOLKS

110G (½ CUP) CASTER SUGAR

2 TBS GROUND ALMONDS

2 TSP DARK COCOA POWDER, PLUS EXTRA FOR DUSTING (SEE NOTE)

¼ TSP GROUND CARDAMOM

2 EGG WHITES

PINCH OF SALT

SPICED PRALINE TUILES (AND JEWELS)

3 TSP CORIANDER SEEDS

1½ TSP CARDAMOM SEEDS

1½ TSP PEPPERCORNS

1 STAR ANISE

1 CINNAMON QUILL

220G (1 CUP) CASTER SUGAR

MANDARIN OIL

60ML (¼ CUP) OLIVE OIL

4 MANDARINS

CRÈME FRAÎCHE, TO SERVE

CHOCOLATE TERRINE

1   Preheat the oven to 160°C. Grease a 25cm x 7cm (base measurement) bar tin and line with baking paper, extending over the two long sides. Place the chocolate and butter into a microwave-safe bowl. Microwave on high for 30 seconds and then stir. Continue to cook in 30-second bursts, stirring in between, until melted and the mixture is smooth. Set aside to cool a little.

2   Place the egg yolks and half the sugar into the bowl of an electric mixer, and beat for 3–4 minutes, until thick and pale. Add the cooled chocolate mixture and mix to combine. Add the ground almonds and the sifted cocoa and cardamom, and mix to combine.

3   In a separate bowl, whisk the egg whites and salt to soft peaks. Gradually add the remaining sugar, a spoonful at a time, until it is all incorporated. Whisk for a further 3 minutes until thick and glossy.

4   Fold a large spoonful of egg white mixture into the chocolate mixture to 'loosen' it, and then fold in the remaining mixture until just combined. Spoon into the prepared tin and cover tightly with foil. Place into a baking dish, and pour in enough boiling water to come halfway up the sides of the tin.

5   Bake for 55 minutes, until the mixture looks set. Remove the tin from the baking dish and cool to room temperature, then refrigerate for about 2 hours, until cold.

SPICED PRALINE

6   Toast the spices one type at a time (they will each take different times to cook) in a dry frying pan over medium heat, until fragrant. Cool. Use a mortar and pestle or spice grinder to grind to a powder, then sift into a bowl and set aside.

→

7 Line a heatproof tray with baking paper. Place the sugar into a medium saucepan, and melt over medium heat, stirring occasionally, until it is a deep, caramel colour. Pour onto the tray and leave for about 15 minutes, to cool and set. Break into pieces and place into a food processor with 1 tablespoon of the spice mixture. Process to a very fine powder. Store remaining spice mixture in an airtight container for future use.

8 Preheat the oven to 200°C. Grease a flat baking tray and line with baking paper. Place a 5cm round cookie cutter onto the tray, and spoon 1 teaspoon of the praline powder into it. Smooth it out with the back of a spoon as much as possible. Carefully lift the cookie cutter away to leave a neat round. Repeat two more times so there are 3 circles on the tray.

9 Bake for 3 minutes. As soon as they come out of the oven use the back of a warm spoon to spread the mixture into a slightly larger circle. You will have to work quickly otherwise it will begin to stick to the spoon! Leave on the tray for about 5 minutes until cool and set. Lift from the paper and set aside. Repeat to make another 3 rounds.

10 Scatter the remaining praline powder in a very fine layer on the baking sheet (you may need to do this in 2 batches, as the layer needs to be very thin). Bake for 3 minutes then allow it to cool completely. Scrape the tiny 'jewels' into a container and set aside.

MANDARIN OIL

11 Pour the olive oil into a small bowl. Rest a fine Microplane zester over the bowl and grate the zest from the mandarins into the bowl, trying to catch as much of the mandarin 'mist' as possible. Cover the bowl with plastic wrap and set aside to infuse for 1 hour.

ASSEMBLING

12 Brush a line of mandarin oil onto each serving plate. Dust the chocolate terrine with sifted cocoa and cut into slices. Place a slice onto one end of the mandarin oil.

13 Place a quenelle of crème fraîche onto the chocolate terrine, and stand a praline tuille in each quenelle. Scatter some praline 'jewels' onto the other end of the mandarin oil.

NOTE

The chocolate terrine, praline and oil can all be made ahead of time and then assembled just prior to serving. Couverture chocolate is very good-quality chocolate, which sets beautifully. It is available from specialty food shops. However, if you can't find it, use any good-quality dark chocolate. Dark cocoa powder is also known as Dutch or Dutch process cocoa. It has a rich deep colour and flavour, and is available from delis and specialty food shops.

Buttered Popcorn Ice Cream with Bitter Caramel and Salted Almond Crumb

This is a bit of a playful dessert, as I've taken a popular movie snack, buttered popcorn, and turned it into an ice cream. Add some bitter caramel and salted almond crumble and you might even feel like a movie star as you sit down to this treat!

PREP TIME: *45 minutes*
COOKING TIME: *45 minutes + setting*
FREEZING TIME: *overnight*
MAKES: *6 serves*

BUTTERED POPCORN ICE CREAM

300ML CREAM

300ML MILK

3 CUPS POPPED BUTTERED MICROWAVE POPCORN

5 EGG YOLKS

110G (½ CUP) CASTER SUGAR

PINCH OF SALT

BITTER CARAMEL SAUCE AND JELLY

220G (1 CUP) CASTER SUGAR

100ML HOT WATER

3 GOLD-STRENGTH GELATINE LEAVES

SALTED ALMOND CRUMBS

75G (½ CUP) PLAIN FLOUR

30G (¼ CUP) ALMOND MEAL

55G (¼ CUP) BROWN SUGAR

FINELY GRATED ZEST OF ½ LEMON

60G COLD BUTTER, CHOPPED

35G (¼ CUP) SLIVERED ALMONDS, TOASTED

1 TSP SEA SALT FLAKES

BUTTERED POPCORN ICE CREAM

1 Place the cream, milk and popcorn in a large saucepan over medium-low heat, and heat until steaming. Remove from the heat, and stand for 15 minutes to infuse. Strain through a sieve and discard the popcorn.

2 Beat the egg yolks and caster sugar in the bowl of an electric mixer on high speed for 3–4 minutes, until thick and pale. Add the salt and mix to combine. Reduce the speed to low, and slowly pour in the strained cream mixture.

3 Transfer (if necessary) to a heatproof bowl that will fit snugly over a saucepan of gently simmering water, ensuring that the bottom of the bowl is not touching the water. Whisk for 3 minutes on low speed, then a further 7–12 minutes on medium speed until the mixture has thickened and reached 85°C (if you don't have a thermometer, the mixture should be too hot to leave your finger in there!).

4 Cool to room temperature, then chill until very cold. You can speed up this process by transferring the mixture to a stainless steel bowl placed over another bowl of ice and a splash of water, and then refrigerating for 2–3 hours, stirring occasionally.

5 Churn in an ice cream machine, according to the manufacturer's instructions. Spoon the churned mixture into a nut roll tin (see Note) and freeze overnight.

BITTER CARAMEL SAUCE AND JELLY

6 Place the sugar into a medium saucepan over medium-low heat and stir occasionally, until the sugar has melted and turned a deep amber colour. Add 50ml hot water, taking care as it will react violently. Add the remaining water and stir to incorporate. If necessary bring it back to a simmer, stirring, to dissolve any lumps that might have formed. (If necessary, strain to remove any stubborn lumps.)

→

7   Soak the gelatine in cold water for 5 minutes, until softened. Measure out 125ml (½ cup) of the caramel syrup and pour back into the saucepan. Set the remainder aside, to use as the sauce. Add an extra 125ml (½ cup) water to the saucepan and heat gently until steaming. Squeeze the excess water from the gelatine and add to the pan. Take off the heat and stir until dissolved. Pour into a shallow metal tin (I used 20cm x 14cm base measurement, but you can use different dimensions, as long as the jelly is about 5mm deep). Refrigerate for about 3 hours, until set.

8   Close to serving time, rest a ruler on the tin edge to use as a guide. Cut the jelly in the tin with a sharp knife, into 5mm dice. Lift out using a palette knife.

SALTED ALMOND CRUMBS

9   Preheat the oven to 170°C, and line a baking tray with baking paper. Combine the flour, almond meal, brown sugar and lemon zest in a mixing bowl. Use your fingertips to rub in the butter until it resembles wet sand. It should hold together when squeezed but also easily crumble again. Stir in the almonds and ½ teaspoon of the salt flakes.

10 Spread the mixture onto the lined baking tray and bake for 15–20 minutes, stirring the crumbs occasionally, until crisp. Remove from the oven and cool on the tray.

11 Place the crumbs into a mortar and pestle and lightly crush until it resembles coarse sand. Stir in the remaining salt. Be aware that this mixture is quite salty and not what I would normally do to crumble, but the dish as a whole needs it for balance.

ASSEMBLING

12 To assemble, place two spoonfuls of the crumbs onto each serving plate and flatten slightly. Drizzle the bitter caramel sauce around the plate in swirls. Dot a few cubes of jelly around the syrup. Remove the ice cream from the nut roll tin and cut a thick slice for each serve, placing it onto the crumble. Top the ice cream with a few more jelly cubes.

NOTE

The ice cream, bitter caramel sauce, jelly and the crumble can all be made ahead of time and then assembled just prior to serving. If you don't have a nut roll tin (which I use because I like the shape), you can just use a loaf tin.

Raspberry and Hazelnut Tarts with Poached Meringue and Frangelico Syrup

These little tarts are delicate in size; however, that is no indication of their flavour – they are packed full of raspberries and hazelnuts, two of my favourite foods!

PREP TIME: *40 minutes*
COOKING TIME: *about 25 minutes*
 + cooling and refrigeration
MAKES: *8*

RASPBERRY AND HAZELNUT TARTS

100G SCOTCH FINGER BISCUITS, ROUGHLY BROKEN

100G HAZELNUTS

75G BUTTER, MELTED

200G RASPBERRIES
(FRESH OR THAWED FROM FROZEN)

JUICE OF ½ LIME

55G (¼ CUP) CASTER SUGAR

2 EGG YOLKS

POACHED MERINGUES

2 EGG WHITES

110G (½ CUP) CASTER SUGAR

500ML (2 CUPS) MILK

FRANGELICO SYRUP

110G (½ CUP) CASTER SUGAR

125ML (½ CUP) WATER

70ML FRANGELICO (SEE NOTE)

LIME JUICE, TO TASTE

CANDIED HAZELNUTS

110G (½ CUP) CASTER SUGAR

8 HAZELNUTS

RASPBERRY AND HAZELNUT TARTS

1 Preheat the oven to 175°C. Grease eight 6.5cm (base measurement) loose-bottom tart tins.

2 For the base, place the biscuits and the hazelnuts into a food processor, and process to fine crumbs. With the motor running, pour in the melted butter and process until evenly moistened. Divide the mixture among the tart tins and use your fingers to press evenly over the base and sides. Refrigerate for about 20 minutes, until firm.

3 For the filling, place the raspberries, lime juice and 1 tablespoon of the sugar into a blender and blend until smooth. Pour through a sieve to remove the seeds. In the bowl of an electric mixer, whisk the egg yolks and remaining sugar together until thick and pale. Add the raspberry puree and whisk until smooth. Pour the mixture onto the firm bases and bake for 15 minutes, until set. Cool to room temperature, then refrigerate until cold.

POACHED MERINGUES

4 Place the egg whites and sugar into a heatproof bowl that fits snugly over a saucepan of simmering water (make sure the base of the bowl doesn't touch the water). Using hand-held electric beaters, whisk the mixture constantly until it becomes the temperature of very hot water. If you have a thermometer it should reach 65°C. If you don't have a thermometer it's the temperature where you can dip your finger in but you wouldn't want to leave it there!

5 Tip the hot mixture into the bowl of an electric stand mixer with the whisk attachment, and whisk on high until it stops steaming. Reduce the speed to medium and whisk until the mixture is just warm. Reduce the speed to low and whisk until the mixture is room temperature. Meanwhile, pour the milk into a medium saucepan and heat until steaming (don't let it boil).

→

6 Using a small ice cream scoop (4cm diameter) dipped into the warm milk, make scoops of meringue and drop them into the steaming milk. Cook for about 2 minutes, until firm to the touch (probably best to do these in 2 batches). Lift out with a lightly oiled slotted spoon and place onto a plate lined with paper towel. Refrigerate until needed.

FRANGELICO SYRUP

7 To make the Frangelico syrup, combine the sugar and water in a small saucepan and stir over medium-low heat until the sugar has dissolved. Add 50ml of the Frangelico, increase the heat and bring to a simmer. Cook for 8–10 minutes, until the mixture is syrupy. Remove from the heat, add the remaining Frangelico and a squeeze of lime juice to taste. Pour into a jug and cool to room temperature.

CANDIED HAZELNUTS

8 Line a heatproof tray with baking paper. Place the sugar into a small saucepan over medium-low heat and cook, stirring occasionally, until melted and golden. Meanwhile, push a sharp skewer into the base of 8 hazelnuts, taking care not to split them (or your hand!).

9 Dip each hazelnut into the caramel and hold it upside down, re-dipping as necessary, until the drip holds and sets. Lay carefully onto the prepared tray and leave for about 10 minutes to set.

ASSEMBLING

10 Remove the tarts from the tins and place onto serving plates. Place a poached meringue onto each tart, and top each meringue with a candied hazelnut. Drizzle the plates with Frangelico syrup.

NOTE

The tarts, meringues and syrup can all be made ahead of time. The tarts and meringues should be stored in the fridge and the syrup stored at room temperature. Frangelico is a hazelnut liqueur.

Conversion chart

OVEN TEMPERATURES

	Celsius	Fahrenheit
Very Slow	120	250
Slow	150	275–300
Moderately Slow	170	325
Moderate	180	350–375
Moderately Hot	200	400
Hot	220	425–450
Very Hot	240	475

NOTE

These measures are a guide for conventional ovens

LIQUID CONVERSIONS

Metric	Imperial
50 ml	2fl oz
125 ml	4fl oz
175 ml	6fl oz
225 ml	8fl oz
300 ml	10fl oz
450 ml	16fl oz
600 ml	20fl oz
1 litre	35fl oz

DRY MEASURES

Metric	Imperial
15 g	½ oz
30 g	1 oz
60 g	2 oz
90 g	3 oz
125 g	4 oz (¼ lb)
155 g	5 oz
185 g	6 oz
220 g	7 oz
250 g	8 oz (½ lb)
280 g	9 oz
315 g	10 oz
345 g	11 oz
375 g	12 oz (¾ lb)
410 g	13 oz
440 g	14 oz
470 g	15 oz
500 g	16 oz (1 lb)
750 g	24 oz (1½ lb)
1 kg	32 oz (2 lb)

LENGTH MEASURES

Metric	Imperial
3 mm	⅛ in
6 mm	¼ in
1 cm	½ in
2 cm	¾ in
2.5 cm	1 in
5 cm	2 in
6 cm	2½ in
8 cm	3 in
10 cm	4 in
13 cm	5 in
15 cm	6 in
18 cm	7 in
20 cm	8 in
23 cm	9 in
25 cm	10 in
28 cm	11 in
30 cm	12 in

Special dietary requirements

GLUTEN-FREE RECIPES

Amaretti
Baked Honey and Rosemary Apples
Baked Vanilla Bean Custards
Balsamic Pavlova with Strawberry Cream
Basic Sugar Syrup
Blood Orange Baked Custard
Caramel Syrup
Caramelised Banana with Toasted Coconut
    Ice Cream and White Chocolate Peanuts
Choc-Dipped Frozen Fruit on a Stick
Chocolate Date and Hazelnut Torte
Chocolate Sauce
Chocolate Sorbet
Crème Anglaise
Dessert Wine Zabaglione
Flourless Almond and Blueberry Cake
Frangelico Zabaglione with White Chocolate
    Hazelnuts and Fresh Figs
Hazelnut Cream Biscuits
Homemade Honeycomb with Grand Marnier
    Chocolate Dipping Sauce
Homemade Ice Magic
Individual Chocolate and Hazelnut Semi-Freddo
Lemon Sorbet
Little Chocolate Meringues
Mango Panna Cotta with Orange Blossom Jelly
No-Churn Mango Sorbet
No-Churn Raspberry Sorbet
Orange Blossom and Pistachio Meringues
Passionfruit Curd
Passionfruit Ice Cream
Passionfruit Meringue Roll
Passionfruit Splice with Pineapple Carpaccio
Peach and Champagne Granita
Peanut and Salted Caramel Sundae
Peanut Butter Ice Cream
Plum and Red Wine Mousse
Real Caramel Sauce
Rhubarb, Vanilla and Almond Semi-Freddo
Rose Raspberry and Pistachio Frozen Nougat
Scorched Honey, Fig and Pecan Frozen Nougat
Simple Caramel Sauce
Simple Vanilla Ice Cream
Special Occasion Vanilla Bean Ice Cream
Spiced Crème Brûlée
Strawberries in Dessert Wine Syrup with
    Crushed Amaretti
Strawberry Mousse
Toasted Coconut Ice Cream
Toffee Apple Sorbet
Tropical Fruit Salad with Lemongrass Syrup
Vincotto Figs With Caramelised Walnuts and
    Mascarpone
Warm Chocolate Pots
Watermelon and Mint Granita with Lime Syrup
White Chocolate and Almond Dessert Cake

DAIRY-FREE RECIPES

Amaretti
Basic Sugar Syrup
Blackcurrant Jelly
Caramel Syrup
Chocolate Sorbet (omit grated chocolate)
Dessert Wine Zabaglione (omit the
    cream)
Frangelico Zabaglione with White
    Chocolate Hazelnuts and Fresh Figs
    (omit the cream)
Homemade Honeycomb (omit the
    Grand Marnier Chocolate Dipping
    Sauce)
Lemon Sorbet
Little Chocolate Meringues
No-Churn Mango Sorbet
No-Churn Raspberry Sorbet
Peach and Champagne Granita
Strawberries in Dessert Wine Syrup
    with Crushed Amaretti
Toffee Apple Sorbet
Tropical Fruit Salad with Lemongrass
    Syrup
Watermelon and Mint Granita with
    Lime Syrup

EGG-FREE RECIPES

Apricot and Thyme Tarte Tatin
Baked Honey and Rosemary Apples
Basic Sugar Syrup
Blackcurrant Jelly
Caramel Syrup
Choc-Dipped Frozen Fruit on a Stick
Chocolate Sauce
Chocolate Sorbet
Crumbly Caramel Peaches and
    Cream
Dipping Sauce
Embarrassingly Simple Chocolate
    Hazelnut Pastries
Flat-Pack Gingerbread Houses
Homemade Honeycomb with
    Grand Marnier Chocolate
Lemon Sorbet
Maggie Beer's Sour Cream Pastry
Mango Panna Cotta with Orange
    Blossom Jelly
Old-Fashioned Apple Pie (omit
    egg wash)
Peach and Champagne Granita
Peanut and Salted Caramel Sundae
Pear, Walnut and Mascarpone
    Galette
Real Caramel Sauce
Rough Puff Pastry
Salted Caramel, Almond and
    Chocolate Slice
Sare's Melting Moments
Simple Caramel Sauce
Toffee Apple Sorbet
Tropical Fruit Salad with
    Lemongrass Syrup (omit the
    mango sorbet)
Vincotto Figs With Caramelised
    Walnuts and Mascarpone
Watermelon and Mint Granita with
    Lime Syrup

Index

Acknowledgements

Life is full of opportunities, but the reality is, the opportunities that have been afforded to me over the past twelve months have come as a direct result of a lot of hard work from people other than me. I feel strongly that this cookbook is a record of all that hard work, and so I want to take this opportunity to acknowledge all the people who have made this possible.

Firstly, I must thank the one who not only made the world, but who also came up with the variety of food in it! God not only sustains my life but He has blessed me beyond my wildest dreams.

None of my 'foodie journey' would have been possible without the self-sacrificial love and endless encouragement from Luke, my husband. Far beyond single handedly coping with endless loads of washing, packing of school lunch boxes, housework, homework and bedtime stories for much of the past twelve months, he is also my confidant, counsellor and closest friend. He always seems to know when I need ideas, accountability, advice ... or just a laugh!

My children, Erin, Liam and Maya, have, quite simply, astounded me! I'm not sure that I would have coped so well as a child as they have with the enormous change to their routine over the past year. They remain so grounded, flexible and patient, and make my life as their mother so rewarding and so full of joy.

My extended family and friends have provided a support network beyond belief! I can't believe that I have been blessed with such generous, loyal and encouraging people around me. Particular mention has to be made to my mother-in-law, Barbara, and my friends Alisa and Kristy, who have gone 'above and beyond' in support of our family, stepping in to help with child-minding and child-transportation.

Of course, I would not even have had the opportunity to write this cookbook without all involved in the production of *MasterChef Australia* 2011. I am so grateful to: the judges, for their willingness to share their knowledge and experiences ... and sense of humour; the producers, for their creativity and care of us; the crew, for their warmth and hard work; and of course the other contestants, who proved to be such a lovely bunch of people to spend time with.

So many people at Random House have worked tirelessly to make the ideas floating around in my head a reality in book form. In particular, I am thankful to: Nikki Christer, who has guided me so proficiently through this process and has always been so available and understanding; Anna Govender, who has kept me on track; Mary Callahan, who has so sensitively and creatively worked to bring my ideas to life on paper; Tracy Rutherford, who kindly scoured my recipes with an experienced eye and was so patient with my inexperience; Philippa Sibley, who apart from being one of the best pastry chefs in the country is someone I now count as a friend; Dan Magree, who not only produces beautiful photographs (even on an iPhone!), but who is also so generous with his time and resources; and Lisa La Barbera, whose creative choices were so in line with what I like. To you all, and the many unnamed people behind the scenes too, I am incredibly grateful.

And finally, but importantly, to you who own the book. Without people like you who share my passion for good food there would be no point in writing a cookbook. I hope you enjoy cooking these recipes as much as I have enjoyed creating them.

An Ebury Press book
Published by Random House Australia Pty Ltd
Level 3, 100 Pacific Highway, North Sydney NSW 2060
www.randomhouse.com.au

First published by Ebury Press in 2012

Addresses for companies within the Random House Group can be found at
www.randomhouse.com.au/offices

National Library of Australia
Cataloguing-in-Publication Entry

Bracks, Kate
The Sweet Life: the basics and beyond / Kate Bracks

ISBN 978 1 86471 136 3 (hbk)

MasterChef (Television program).
Cooking. Australian.

641.5994

Art direction and design by Mary Callahan Design
Photography by Dan Magree Photography
Styling by Lisa La Barbera
Food Editing by Tracy Rutherford
Recipe Preparation by Philippa Sibley
Index by Puddingburn Publishing Services
Printed and bound by Everbest Printing Co Ltd. Printed in China

The publisher would like to thank Marilyn and Alastair Sinclair for allowing
us to use their beautiful kitchen.